CHANGE YOUR THINKING, CHANGE YOUR LIFE

Home Study Course

in the

SCIENCE OF MIND

By

ERNEST HOLMES

With Appendixes by Reginald C. Armor

VOLUME ONE

Science of Mind Publications

Los Angeles, California

© 1984 by Science of Mind Publications
ISBN 0-911336-92-3 (Volume One)
ISBN 0-911336-91-5 (Complete six-volume set)

TABLE OF CONTENTS

VOLUME ONE

LESSON 1

CREATION

The Life Principle and Creative Cause

A Message from Ernest Holmes

You are about to start on the most interesting quest the human mind has ever made, the discovery of the Life Principle, the way It works, and your relationship to It. You are about to make the greatest discovery of your life, which is how to use the Creative Power of your thought for definite purposes; purposes which will benefit you, your family, and your friends.

The lessons which follow are not a revelation to some particular individual nor to any one group of persons. Rather they are an outcome or a putting together of the best that the ages have discovered. We all believe that there is a Power greater than we are. We all hope that we may be able to use this Power.

Throughout the ages certain individuals have discovered some secret relationship between themselves and the Universe which other people have not known about, and because of this they have either consciously or unconsciously used a power that to the ordinary individual seems miraculous because of its effects. Others have stood in awe before them, feeling that God has delivered some message to them which is withheld from others.

This age of superstition, of fear and ignorance is passing out of existence, and intelligent people are beginning to say, "My relationship to God, to the Universe, and to the Power which is greater than I am must be as immediate to me as to any other person who ever lived. There is a secret, the great secret of Life Itself, and I expect to discover it. And when I do I know that it will be immediate and personal to me; something that I can live by and use; something that I can benefit by and demonstrate; something that will take the uncertainties out of life."

You are about to engage in a study of the Science of Mind, which deals with a Principle and a Power in the Universe as immediate as your own breath. Of necessity such a study is something to which you must give your complete attention, something that you must enthusiastically enter into. All the while it will be something that brings a daily satisfaction, a sense of well-being, and the gratification of knowing that you are in league with the Power that creates and sustains everything.

These lessons start with the simple proposition that God, which means the Life Principle or the Creative Cause, is an immediate Presence not only around but within you. Therefore do not be afraid that perhaps you are being coerced into accepting a new religion, for such is not the case. You, like all normal people, already believe in some Power greater than you are. You already understand that everything in the Universe is governed by some invisible law, force, and intelligence which sanity compels you to accept, and you are going to discover your immediate relationship to this Power, to establish yourself in such conscious unity with It that you too will become a partner in Its activities.

You should approach your study with a calm determination and a buoyant hope. We believe that as you study these lessons and the various explanations that go with them you will find yourself agreeing with their content and meaning. You may be certain that this meaning has been accepted by the deep thinkers of every age.

In presenting such a vast subject as this it is necessary that there be considerable repetition. The ideas must be presented in many forms for clarity. We hope that you will begin at once to apply these lessons. If you do, long before your studies are finished you will have demonstrated that there is a Power greater than you are and you can use It.

Your first lesson starts on page 63 of The Science of Mind *Textbook and runs to the top of page 68. You will get the best results if you faithfully follow the Textbook with each lesson, explaining to yourself the meaning of each paragraph and each word.*

The Glossary at the end of the Textbook will give you the information you need in conjunction with these lessons.

Starting with this lesson and running through Lesson 12 is an explanation of the inner meaning of the Bible. This explanation is based on what we consider the finest authority. With each lesson you will find supplementary material on specific subjects which are of great importance in coming to comprehend the whole meaning of this course.

While our first lesson starts with page 63, it will be well for you to study the whole Introductory Section of The Science of Mind *Textbook from Page 25 to 60 inclusive. The sum and substance of this section of our Textbook resolves itself into this: The Universe is made up of a Divine Infinite Presence, an Intelligence and supreme Spirit which responds to everyone because It is incarnated in everyone. This response is immediate and personal. The Universe is also a system of Law and Order, and you are surrounded by a Creative Principle which responds to the impress of your thought and acts upon it exactly as you think. These are the great realities with which we deal.*

And now you are ready to start on your adventure. We believe it will be a happy one.

CREATION

The Life Principle and Creative Cause

(textbook reference: pages 63-68)

Let us make plain exactly what we mean by *In the Beginning God.* Of course we do not mean that there ever was a time when God began to be or when the Creative Cause first started to function. What we really mean is the beginning of any created thing.

For instance, in the springtime of the year when the farmer sows his grain means *in the beginning,* before his crop is created by the laws of nature. In the beginning, then, means any springtime of causation, before any particular object is created.

It is impossible to suppose any beginning to Reality Itself. The Ancient of Days referred to in the Bible never began. This Reality, to which we have given the name God, is an ever-present fact in every man's experience.

This Infinite and Universal Creative Spirit is Intelligence, Imagination, Knowingness, coupled with an Infinite Law which executes the Self-knowingness of Spirit. The entire Introductory Section of our Textbook, *The Science of Mind,* up to page 60, is a simplified exposition of the theory that there is a Creative Intelligence that knows, and a Universal Law that obeys the will of this Creative Intelligence.

It is impossible to explain life without starting with the proposition that Reality or some final Truth already exists; that behind everything which takes form there is an Intelligence that creates all forms. Now within this Intelligence must exist the potentiality or the possibility of everything that is to follow, which is but another way of saying that God is Absolute Intelligence, Limitless Imagination, Perfect Consciousness, and Complete Self-expression.

CREATION

In the beginning nothing exists other than this Absolute Intelligence. The Bible refers to the Spirit as moving. If we have an Infinite Intelligence that moves, It must move upon Itself since there is nothing outside Itself. All movement, then, is an interior movement. All creation is a result of this interior movement of the Life Principle upon Itself.

We must assume that the pattern for Its movement, the impulse toward self-expression, the idea, or if we choose to call it the thought, exists in the Mind of God before ever it is formed into objective fact. That is what is meant at the top of page 84 in our Textbook where it says: *Spirit makes things out of Itself through some inner act upon Itself.* This inner act must be an act of consciousness, an act of thought or idea. This inner Consciousness moves upon Itself; that is, It thinks or knows within Itself. Within Its own nature there is a Law obeying Its will.

You will learn later that this Law is the Law we use in what we call *demonstration*. By demonstration we mean bringing some good into our personal experience which we have desired but have not yet experienced. You will learn that we all take part in this original creative act; that man, because of his nature, cannot stop creating; it is merely a question of what we wish to create or have created for us.

This inner movement of the Spirit upon Itself we call self-contemplation. Since we shall speak a great deal about self-contemplation it is well to analyze exactly what we mean by it. Self-contemplation is an inner awareness, an inner sense of being, and this inner awareness in God must of course be complete. Therefore God must forever be expressed, and God's expression must always be harmonious and perfect because God is harmonious and perfect.

If someone should ask how we know that God must be harmonious and perfect our answer would be that it is a self-evident proposition that if the original Creative Cause were anything other than perfect It would be self-destructive. No matter which way we look at this or how often we turn it over for re-examination, we shall always be impelled to return to the self-evident starting point that the Truth is that which is; that there is an Eternal Reality which makes things out of Itself by becoming what It makes.

When we read the story of creation we should realize that we are reading the

CREATION

thoughts of someone who, like ourselves, attempted to put into words what creation meant to him. He arrived at the self-evident proposition that there is an original Creative Cause. He also asserted that this original Creative Cause must work through Self-knowingness. He described the result of God's thought as a perfect and harmonious creation or manifestation of the Infinite Harmony, the Infinite Wholeness. Naturally he had to put his ideas into human language, as we all must, and in so doing made rather a human narrative, which is also necessary. It is impossible for us to talk unless we use words to symbolize our meaning.

All words are symbols, and when we use the words *First Cause, Absolute Intelligence, God, Spirit,* or *Reality,* they are but vehicles conveying the meaning back of the words, and in this instance the meaning is that there must be, and is, a Universal Creative Intelligence which was never born, which never came into being, but which always existed.

While you and I with our finite minds do not grasp the significance of Infinite Being, certainly not in Its entirety, we do understand something of Its meaning, and out of the little that we grasp are born such ideas of God as we possess. From the great and inspired literature of the ages and from many findings in scientific research we are led to the legitimate and justifiable conclusion that God is an Omnipresent Reality; that this Creative Cause which produces all form also exists at the center of our own being, carrying on Its creative work in us; that we are co-partners in Its Infinitude, some part of Its Eternal Reality.

Jesus simplified it in these words: *The words that I speak unto you, I speak not of myself: but the Father, that dwelleth in me, he doeth the works.* He meant that the same Creative Intelligence which gives form to all things also worked in him, and through him gave form to substance, therefore he said that the very words which he spoke were Spirit and they were Life.

You will discover that a spiritual interpretation of the Science of Mind leads to the acceptance of the thought that the Creative Spirit works in and through each one of us, that the Power which we seek we already possess, and that the recognition of this Power is certain to demonstrate the reality of Its presence through a betterment in all outward circumstances. These are the tools we use, and most amazing results are obtained when they are used definitely and for specific purposes.

Now the *Word of God* means the consciousness of God doing something. It is God in the act of creation. I am sure that we all believe that God is in and through all people and all things. As a matter of fact there is nothing else that we could be made of, is there, except God?

On page 393 you will find these words: *The correct understanding that Mind in Its unformed state can be called forth into individual use is the key to all proper mental and spiritual work from a practical viewpoint.* This means that every time we think we use the energy of God. And on page 414: *Thoughts are more than things, they are the cause of things.*

The Self-contemplation of God referred to on page 64 means the Thought of God; and the Story of Creation on pages 64 and 65 needs no further elaboration. For a clear understanding read these pages carefully several times and put a great deal of thought into their true meaning. While the narrative seems rather human, remember that we are putting into human language that which can only be imagined.

The paragraph on page 66 under the heading, *Describing the Infinite,* explains that God or Spirit is the final answer to all inquiries into the nature of the Universe. Every science has a principle governing it. This principle and the way it works is what science studies. The purpose of philosophy is to inquire into the nature of Reality, while religion is an expression of our belief in God.

You will notice we come to the idea of Absolute Intelligence. Let us examine the meaning of the word *Absolute* as defined in our Glossary on page 575: *The Unconditioned — that which nothing can limit.* Again on page 390 we find these words: *The mind of man is some part of the Mind of God, therefore it contains within itself unlimited possibility of expansion and self-expression.*

You see, then, that Absolute Intelligence means the limitless power of self-expression. There is a Principle of Mind at the very center of our own thought which is infinite in Its ability and limitless in Its power and ever available to us. When we call upon this inner self we are at the same time calling upon God, and when we call upon God we are calling upon this inner self. For both God and man emerge in a complete unity of Mind and Spirit. This is the great secret of all the ages, and you will at once recognize that to have a true and comprehensive understanding of this is exactly what you, and all of us, are seeking.

To understand the meaning of this is your object in taking this course, and to be able to use the Power that already is within you is the thing in which you are interested. We all wish more power, greater happiness, more beauty in our lives, and a greater sense of security. There is something within us which is always whispering to our inner ear that all these things are for us.

The great quest of man has been to solve the riddle of the Universe and see where he, himself, fits into the great design. Knowledge alone can guarantee freedom, and self-recognition can produce knowledge. Is it not true that all knowledge comes from the inner perception of our relationship to the Universe?

Next you will notice these words in paragraph 4, page 66: *Creation means the giving of form to the Substance of Mind or Spirit.* In other words, creation is not making something out of nothing, but rather the giving of form to something that already exists. The electric light is a manifestation of an energy which already exists. The energy is not depleted by using it. No matter how much we use there is still just as much left as there was before we made use of it. There is no limit to the amount that can be generated.

There is a creative energy at the very center of your thought waiting to be called into manifestation. To learn how to use this creative principle is the whole purpose of your study. When the artist paints he gives form to his thought through the medium of his brush and oils. He produces different manifestations of pigments. So in our thoughts we use a creative power by drawing out the latent possibilities of the great Mind in which we live and which finds expression through us.

When the Spirit creates form out of Itself, at the same time It creates space, for as you can plainly see, form is outline while space is the physical distance between any two forms. If there were no forms there would be no space. Both exist in the great Mind of God as means to His Self-expression. They exist in our minds also, because we too are some part of the Universe in which we are living.

If you draw two lines on a blackboard you also create the space existing between these two lines. But if these two particular forms or lines remained uncreated, then the space which might exist between them would have no existence.

Let us avoid confusion by saying that both space and form are created by the action of the thought of God upon Himself. And let us hasten to add that we also are created in the image, mentally and spiritually, of the Great Spirit. You will at once see that it is because of this that your thought is creative. In other words, your thought is creative not because you will it to be so but because it is so. You will learn later that the will is directive only; it is the conviction and the feeling that are the real creative qualities in our minds.

If form creates space in order that form may be outlined and experienced, then does it not follow that the ideas which give rise to form and space must automatically create time? For time is merely the process of duration in which we experience any given form or forms. This is just another way of saying that time, space, and form are primarily mental concepts.

To understand this is to see how it is that new conditions can be created for us by the invisible Principle which we call Mind or Spirit. We know that the Power we all seek to use is not limited by any present form nor in any present form, nor is It limited by any element of time. What a wonderful thing for us to realize! We may use a Power which makes new conditions and new situations; and when It does this It also creates all the things necessary to our well-being.

So we come to the conclusion that Spirit, or God, is forever making and remaking time, space, and form, as you and I are forever thinking some kind of thought. Just as we are always aware of ourselves and of our environment, so there is a greater Mind which is aware of all things. The past, the present, and the future flow from this Mind as a result of the creative activity of Its thought.

On page 495 under the heading, *The Mind that Jesus Used,* you will find these words: *We are to let the mind be in us which was in Christ Jesus.* This means the Mind of God. And on the following page are the words: *This Mind is God working in and through us. God can work* for *us only by working* through *us.* To understand this is to partake of the Divine Nature and to make conscious use of the same Power to which Jesus had access.

CREATION

When we come to inquire into the many different great systems of religious thought which have been given to the world, we shall find that this is the central theme of most of them. Man's thought is creative because his thought is God-Power flowing through his individual will and imagination. That is why it is true that *as a man thinketh in his heart so is he.*

SUMMARY

Let us sum up our first lesson and see what we have discovered:

First: There is a Creative Power in the Universe that manifests Itself through imagination, will, and feeling.

Second: This Creative Power makes things out of Itself by Itself becoming the thing that It makes.

Third: As the Creative Mind of the Universe operates upon Itself through Its will, imagination, and feeling, It creates forms which are subject to It and to Its laws, but which have no reality apart from the Mind which creates them.

Fourth: This Creative Mind is the mind that Jesus used and that we may all use for conscious purposes just as soon as we come to understand how.

This means that everyone is surrounded by the original Creative Intelligence of the Universe. This Intelligence fills all space, flows through everything and is everything. Therefore there is an intelligence in everything that responds to your thinking. You did not make it this way and you cannot change it. This is the nature of your being and of all being. Consequently by impressing your thought upon It you cause It to do something for you, but whether or not you know it you are always impressing your thought upon It because most of your thought is unconscious and flows out into this Creative Intelligence as a stream of thought which we call the Law of Mind in Action. You are, then, surrounded by a Creative Stuff which makes things out of Itself through the simple act of Itself becoming what It makes.

But this same Principle is also in you and is your mind. You are a center of consciousness or self-knowingness in It. Your mind is some part of It. It is not separate from you. Consequently when you think within and upon yourself, you are thinking within and upon It. This puts the use of this Mind Principle in the only place where It could possibly benefit you, and that is within yourself. This is why Jesus said that there is a truth which known will automatically demonstrate itself. We can know only within our own minds. But here within ourselves is our share of the Universal Mind, the One Power, the One Presence, which is God.

QUESTIONS

Brief answers to these questions should be written out by the student after studying this lesson, and the answers compared with those in the Appendix.

1. What do we mean by the phrase, *In the beginning God?*

2. In the Science of Mind how do we define God?

3. What do we mean by a creative series through which anything is brought into being?

4. Can an effect ever be the cause of another creative series?

5. When we speak of God as First Cause what do we mean?

6. Can we contact and use First Cause?

7. What is meant by the Spirit of God?

8. Can we say that man partakes of this Spirit of God? If so, how?

9. Does the Spirit within man grow and develop?

10. How can a person use this Principle of Spirit which is within him to definitely direct the course of his life?

METAPHYSICAL INTERPRETATIONS OF THE BIBLE

based on

Thomas Troward's *Bible Mystery and Bible Meaning*

Thomas Troward, late Divisional Judge, Punjab, India, is recognized as one of the greatest authorities on the subject of Mental Science. His sincerity, the lucidity and profundity of his thought, his great ability to make the complex simple, his profound faith and complete devotion to truth, made him a rare messenger of God.

Troward opens his *Bible Mystery and Bible Meaning* by saying, *The Bible Is the Book of the Emancipation of Man.*

We all remember that Jesus admonished his followers: *Be ye therefore perfect, even as your Father which is in heaven is perfect.* He had already located the Kingdom of Heaven within. Moses affirmed that there is a creative word in our own mouth which is the arbiter of our fate. Again we are told that we shall decree a thing and it will happen; that our word will not return unto us void but that it shall accomplish and prosper.

Troward tells us that these promises are based on the idea of our acquiring a certain type of information. Jesus declared that it depends on our keeping his sayings; Job said that it depends on a right interpretation of the meaning of some law or presence in nature; and Moses said that the gift which he offered his followers would be either a blessing or a curse, according to whether or not they kept the Commandments.

Just what do these sayings mean, and what are these Commandments? It is evident that they must have something to do with Universal Truth and our relationship to It. The Bible begins with the simple proposition that the Creative Intelligence of the Universe, which it calls God, is pure, evenly-distributed Spirit, Mind, or Intelligence. The only instrument of Mind is the movement of Its Intelligence within Itself. This we call *thought* or *contemplation.* The Bible clearly states that creation is the result of the Word of God.

BIBLE MYSTERY AND BIBLE MEANING

The Bible assumes a Law of Mind through which Creative Intelligence works to produce form, thus giving us a trinity which we call *The Thing, the Way It Works, and What It Does.* From beginning to end the Bible teaches that everything which happens in our lives depends on an understanding of the right relationship between the Universe and ourselves. It assumes that just as God, or the Creative Spirit, is a Trinity, so is man a trinity: spirit, soul, and body. In other words man is a microcosm within a macrocosm; a little world within a big world. He partakes of the nature of the Creative Principle. This is neither by preference nor by compulsion. Thought is creative not because we will it so but because it is its nature to be creative.

The Bible teaches what might be called a law of parallels. That is, the physical universe is an out-picturing of a mental universe; laws of mind are just as tangible as are laws of physics. Of course both are invisible. The invisible is always the cause of the visible. Spirit passes from the Universal into an individualized consciousness. Whatever form the consciousness of Spirit takes it is always in accord with One Primary Law: *The Word was made flesh, and dwelt among us.*

No matter what individualized states of consciousness may be produced in the process of evolution, each individual consciousness is a center of God Consciousness. Hence the individual consciousness is the Consciousness of God operating at the level of the individual's comprehension of life. This is fundamental to all Bible teaching: God is One, and man is made in the image and likeness of God.

The Bible has another unique and interesting presentation which Troward calls the *Law of Selectivity* and to which Jesus referred when he said, . . . *as thou hast believed, so be it done unto thee.* The understanding of these two propositions is simple enough when we have the key to their meaning. We are immersed in an Infinite Spirit which stimulates our imagination to the act of thought. We are also immersed in a Universal Law which, acting creatively upon our thought, presents to us conditions that correspond to such states of thought.

So far as we are concerned this means that wherever we set up a center for thought action, there we are automatically reflecting mental images into the Law. The Law always tends to give form to our thought. From the effects of this creative power of thought we shall never escape.

BIBLE MYSTERY AND BIBLE MEANING

When the Bible speaks of the beginning of creation it is referring to an Eternal Beginning and not to some historic time in the cosmos when the Creative Spirit first began to project form. It refers rather to the beginning of any creation; to any seedtime which precedes its following harvest season. Thus Troward tells us that the beginning is a continuous fact, always present, and not to be conceived of as something which has been left behind and done with. It means that previous to any created form there is a universal, equally-distributed Mind, Intelligence, or Spirit. This Mind is the potential of all form. There is a Law of Mind acted upon by idea; hence the movement of consciousness as thought is Law.

In the beginning was the Word, and the Word was with God, and the Word was God. Again let us remember that this beginning is now, in the moment in which we give our mental treatment for the betterment of circumstances for ourselves or others. There is nothing but God, nothing for us but immutable Law and our own thought. Our thought operating through Law will create the desired form if we permit it to do so. This is the fundamental proposition which the Bible sets before us.

When the Bible refers to the heaven and the earth, it is referring to the unformed and the formed. Jesus placed the Kingdom of Heaven within us, which means within our spiritual perception. The earth is likened to the outward form, to that which is created, to objective conditions, circumstances, situations, etc.

We must then consider a Self-evolving Power as the basic Principle of the teachings of the Bible — Something which makes things out of Itself by the very simple and direct act of Itself becoming the thing It makes.

We are told that the earth was without form and that the Spirit moved upon this formlessness, which the Bible likens to *the face of the waters*. The waters of themselves do not move; they are moved upon by the Spirit. This means the movement of thought upon Substance; the movement of Idea as Law into form. We are surrounded by *the waters,* that is, by a universal pool of unformed Substance ready to be moved upon.

This unformed, creative Substance has been likened to the Feminine Principle in nature, the Soul of the Universe as distinguished from the Divine Spirit of the Universe. The Spirit has been called the Masculine and the Soul the Feminine, because it is the projective act of thought moving upon the receptive Principle of Mind which sets creation in motion.

Water is a most interesting symbol as used in the Bible, and indeed in most of the sacred scriptures. In the Upanishads we find this saying: *In the beginning this (world) was water.* From one of the ancient Papyri we read: *I am the great God Who created Himself, which is to say, I am water.* Plutarch says: *Homer, like Thales, had learned from the Egyptians that water was the beginning and origin of all things.* From ancient Babylon we note that *water and earth were to be formed.* This refers to the liquid and the solid in the universe. In the Cabala we find: *The emanation which produced the creation of the universe is like water gushing out from its source and spreading over everything near.* We are told that water is the first element in the mundane system of the Chinese. Paul Deussen, in his *Philosophy of the Upanishads*, says, *This earth, the air, the heavens, the mountains, gods and men . . . are nothing but the water under solid conditions.* This refers to the invisible fluidic cause back of what appears to be a solid creation.

The turning of water into wine is symbolic of the transmutation of lower forms into higher ones. Water is used to symbolize the action of a passive principle which gives form to that which, of itself, has no form. Hence all forms or created things are placed in the category of effects or results. The Absolute Cause is the Creative Intelligence of the Spirit which moves upon the face of the waters; the Masculine Principle impregnating the Feminine with the Divine Ideas.

Troward tells us: *Thus creation is described as the self-transforming action of the One unanalyzable Spirit passing by successive transitions into all the varieties of manifestations that fill the universe.* And when we realize that we ourselves are some part of the Creative Principle we shall see that our thought is always passing into the varieties of manifestation that fill our universe.

Since this is true, man's mind becomes a reproduction of the Divine Mind operating on the scale of individual perception, and Troward tells us: *It is precisely here that the difficulty comes in.* Since we cannot escape the creative power of our thought we must temporarily be limited to such thought patterns as we have already created.

Freedom and expansion lie not in a changed attitude toward us on the part of the Universe or of God, but in a changed mental attitude in our own consciousness, a new outlook upon life, a new vision of Reality.

WHAT IS THE SCIENCE OF MIND?

The Science of Mind as taught in these lessons is an outgrowth of the spiritual faith which people have had throughout the ages. Before science was conceived the Presence of God was felt. Before ever mental actions or reactions were analyzed history was filled with instances of men and women who had experienced God.

The Science of Mind is comparatively new, but the mental experience of the Invisible Universe is as old as the history of man. It is new in that for the first time in history we have put together all findings which contribute to the establishment of man's relationship with the Universe, to the end that he may be able to apply his spiritual understanding to the everyday problems of human life.

This science necessarily starts with the proposition that we are living in a Spiritual Universe whose sole government is one of Harmony, and that the use of right ideas is the enforcement of its Law.

The Science of Mind is built on the theory that there is One Infinite Mind which of necessity includes all that is, whether it be the intelligence in man, the life in the animal, or the invisible Presence which is God. In it we learn to have a spiritual sense of things. This spiritual sense of things is what is meant by the Consciousness of Christ. To be able to discern the spiritual idea back of its physical symbol is to use the mind that Jesus used.

The Science of Mind is intensely practical because it teaches us how to use the Mind Principle for definite purposes, such as helping those who are sick, impoverished, or unhappy. Each one of us should learn to become a practitioner of this science, a demonstrator of its Principle, a conscious user of its Power. Power already exists, but the existence of Power is of no particular value to us until we use it. We must not only be conscious of Power, but we must be actively conscious of it. This is one of the first lessons we learn in the Science of Mind.

WHAT IS THE SCIENCE OF MIND?

This science is more than mental; it is also spiritual, since we live in a Spiritual Universe. The Science of Mind declares the Truth about this Spiritual Universe and it also declares the Truth about false belief, considering everything which is opposed to Good as an accumulation of human thought, the collective negative suggestion of the race.

Wrong conditions are resolved into false beliefs, and through the use of right ideas a transformation of thought takes place. We learn to build our ideas upon an affirmative rather than a negative factor. To state the Truth and deny or disregard that which in belief is opposed to it, is to prove that the Principle of the Science of Mind is actual.

The ever-increasing thousands of persons who are daily proving this Principle add to our conviction that we are dealing with the most intense reality the human mind has ever conceived. As you will learn later, the practice of this science is the application of a definite technique, the law of right thought, of true spiritual understanding.

It is necessary to start these studies with the complete conviction that there is such a Principle and that you understand the scientific use and application of it. Conscious knowledge alone gives you the conscious control of the laws of nature. The advance in any science always corresponds to the conscious use made of the laws of nature. There could be no advance in science without such conscious use of nature's laws.

It would be unwise to approach a study of the Science of Mind with superstition. You must approach it with understanding. Above all, you must approach it with the definite intention in mind of making conscious use of its Principle. You must come to realize at the very start of your inquiry that Mind exists as a Principle in the Universe, just as electricity exists as a principle.

Once you understand this it will not be difficult to see that thought is the tool of Mind, that right ideas enforce the Law of Mind; nor will it be difficult to see that physical objects are fundamentally spiritual in their nature, that an objective fact is but a symbol of a subjective or an invisible cause. It certainly follows that if you are to make practical use of the Science of Mind you must be able to convert things into thoughts, and by changing the stream of consciousness produce a corresponding change in an objective situation, whether this be used for helping those who are sick, or to meet any other need.

The question naturally arises whether man has a right to use his thought for whatever purpose he wills. The more sincere one is the more likely he is to ask this question. Strangely enough, he would not ask this relative to any other science but would feel that all laws exist to be used, and any sane person would naturally desire to benefit himself and others through the use of nature's laws. Why should any exception be made to the greatest of all laws — the Law of Mind in Action, and the enforcement of this Law through right ideas?

One of our fundamental propositions is that God is all there is. When you say God is all there is, that includes everything, all possibility and all action, for Spirit is the invisible essence and substance of all form. It is impossible to separate the highest use of this science from the most exalted conception of an immanent Spirit, a transcendent Spirit, an available Spirit.

Perhaps one might at first have an aversion to the idea of using spiritual power for material purposes, but in the Science of Mind we discover that there are no final material purposes; that whether life exists in an objective or a subjective state, whether it is visible or invisible, all is Spirit; that Spirit or Intelligence, plus what It does, constitutes the entire Universe, including man.

The Science of Mind reveals that every man is a potential Christ. Every man has inherent God-Power within him. And how could this God-Power be used other than through his thought? Since it would be imposssible for a man to act as an intelligent being unless he could first think, the very idea of man supposes a center of consciousness, a center of thought activity. The Science of Mind reveals that this center of God-activity within each one is a complete and unique manifestation of the Parent Mind; that the Power of God does actually exist in man.

It is a basic proposition in our philosophy that we live in a Mental or Spiritual Universe and that things can be resolved into thoughts. This is the foundation upon which all scientific practice must be established, and when you are able to establish this premise in your own thought, you at once find yourself equipped with an instrument through which you can change your environment.

The Science of Mind does not deny the physical universe. The objective universe is the Body of God. That Body includes our physical being. In reality every idea of our physical being is a Divine idea.

The misconception of the Spiritual Universe causes our universe to appear separated from good, and in fact we experience this separation. But that which is a fact in experience is not necessarily true in principle. Bondage cannot be conceived by the Divine, and yet we all know that bondage is a part of man's experience.

In trying to seek a solution for this enigma we must either conclude that there is an ultimate good and an ultimate evil in the universe, or we must conclude that there is but one Ultimate, which is Good, and that this Ultimate by Its very nature and by our very nature is compelled to appear to each one of us in the form of our belief. If you can accept this proposition it will be easy enough for you to see how it is that false belief binds humanity.

If that which binds is false belief and not the Truth, then you will see why Jesus told us that a knowledge of the Truth would produce freedom. He did not mean that knowledge of the Truth creates freedom, but that knowledge of the Truth makes us free by aligning us with that which was never bound.

If we accept the foregoing conclusions as true it follows that the Divine Creative Principle is already perfect, having neither confusion nor chaos within It. It was, is, and will remain exactly perfect. Our individual universe shall be redeemed from its bondage in such degree as we become actively conscious of the Truth of our being. We must use the Law as a Law of Liberty, else we shall be using It as a law of bondage.

The Science of Mind provides us with a definite technique for the use of this Law and teaches how each one can use It in freeing himself and demonstrating to his complete satisfaction that right ideas, correctly used, can and must produce right conditions.

So far, science, revelation, and philosophy have arrived at no conclusion which could disturb this proposition, and every day the physical sciences are more completely proving that the physical universe in which we live is more like a *gigantic thought* than anything else. Now if the physical universe, or the cosmos as a whole, is more like a gigantic thought than anything else, it follows that our immediate world is a part of this thought.

How amazed we all should be if we awoke some fine morning, not only with the absolute conviction that this is so, but also with the inner insight which would enable us to see exactly what it means. Then we too should be able to say to the paralyzed man, "Stretch forth thine hand!" But before we can do this we must see the principle of freedom instead of the belief in a paralysis of this principle.

The Science of Mind is a reinterpretation of the Universe by a process of thought which Jesus used. We learn that there is one body, the body of right ideas. Jesus sensed this Body of God, which includes man's body, as a perfect, harmonious unit, and he realized that the evil which binds man is not a principle within itself nor a thing of itself, and most certainly not a person, but merely a false system of thought. He understood that his knowledge of good annihilated that which denied good. This fundamental fact he clearly brought out in his teaching; the Truth known is followed by the Truth demonstrated.

The Science of Mind does not necessarily create a new religion or sect, for it may be added to any spiritual system of thought since it is a complement to all. The person who already has the greatest spiritual faith will make the most active demonstrator of Truth. The person who naturally has a spiritual insight or who has already trained himself to have spiritual insight, will more quickly sense the truths which the Science of Mind portrays. He will more quickly lay hold of its technique and more perfectly demonstrate for himself and others that the Invisible is the cause of the visible.

For every science there must be a technique or a way of proving its truth. Science of itself is a knowledge of laws and principles and systematic arrangement. And the technique of any science is the way in which we use this knowledge of laws and principles.

Applying this rule (which is common to all sciences) to the Science of Mind, it naturally follows that if there is such a principle as Universal Mind, and if It does work according to the Law of Cause and Effect, and if thought, self-contemplation, or self-knowingness is that which stimulates Its action, then correct thinking can and must produce objective or visible results.

We must lay even more stress on the *use* of the Science of Mind than we do on seeking to establish its Principle. As a matter of fact its Principle is self-evident; its use is exactly what we make it. And the first thing that any student of this science should do is determine to make daily use of it. In this, as in all other things, we should be practical. Too much study of any principle without making conscious use of it will lead to mere theorizing, and I am sure we all wish practical results.

You are ready to use the Principle governing the Science of Mind the very moment you accept the fact that there is such a principle and that it does operate through your thought. But this seems to be the place where many fall down. They talk so much about the Principle and use It so little. They permit themselves to become confused by the introduction of contradictory ideas. They spend too much time in merely philosophizing, theorizing, speculating, until finally they live in a world of wistful wishing, of day dreams.

You must come to see that the Science of Mind is an actual Principle to be definitely used; that no matter how much Good may exist in the Universe, only as much Good can come to you as you can conceive. Above all things, determine now to use this science. Do not say, "Well, this is but the first lesson and I expect to have understanding enough within a year to use it." Seize upon whatever facts present themselves to your mind today, begin to use such truth as you grasp out of your first lesson, and before the year is over you will have become an effective practitioner.

HOW TO GIVE A SPIRITUAL TREATMENT

You may as well begin right now to use the Science of Mind for practical purposes to help yourself and your friends or to change any condition which needs to be improved.

So why not choose one or two persons or conditions, and using the following instructions, take a definite time each day for a period of treatment. If you do this I am certain that before you finish this course you will have discovered the secret of secrets and you will have demonstrated the greatest truth ever discovered.

For *Physical Healing*

Take a definite time at least twice each day to be alone, sit down, compose your mind, and think about God. Try to arrive at a deep sense of peace and calm. Then assume an attitude of faith in a Power greater than you are.

Say: *The words I speak are the Law of Good and they will produce the desired result because they are operated on by a Power greater than I am. Good alone goes from me and good alone returns to me.*

You are now ready to give a specific treatment for yourself. Begin by saying: *This word is for myself. Everything I say is for me and about me. It is the truth about my real self.* (You are thinking about your spiritual nature, the Divine Reality of yourself, the God in you.) Say: *There is One Life, that Life is God, that Life is perfect, that Life is my life now.* Say this slowly and with deep meaning.

Next say: *My body is a manifestation of the Living Spirit. It is created and sustained by the One Presence and the One Power. That Power is flowing in and through me now, animating every organ, every action and every function of my physical being. There is perfect circulation, perfect assimilation, and perfect elimination. There is no congestion, no confusion, and no inaction. I am one with the In-*

finite Rhythm of life, which flows through me in love, in harmony, and in peace. There is no fear, no doubt, and no uncertainty in my mind. I am letting that Life which is perfect flow through me and become my life. It is my life now. There is One Life, that Life is God, that Life is perfect, that Life is my life now.

Next, deny everything that contradicts this. Follow each denial with a direct affirmation of its opposite. In a certain sense you are presenting a logical argument to your own mind, based on the belief that there is but One Life, which is perfect and which is your life now. The evidence that you bring out in your argument should reach a conclusion which causes your own mind to accept the verdict of perfection. Remember you are not talking about your physical body as though it were separate from the spirit, but about God in you; therefore you will have no difficulty in convincing yourself that this God in you is perfect.

You have now reached a place of realization in which you enter into a feeling of assurance that comes from a consciousness of the Divine Presence in, around, and through you. This period of realization should last for several moments, during which you sit quietly accepting the meaning of what you have said. Then say: *It is now done. It is now complete. It is now perfect. There is One Life, that Life is God, that Life is perfect, that Life is my life now.*

Between these periods of meditation try to keep your mind poised in such a way that you do not contradict what you have said in your treatment. Keep your mind open at all times to a Divine influx of new inspiration, new power, and new life. Accept what you have said with joy and gratitude.

For *Betterment of Conditions*

In treating for the betterment of conditions you are using the same Principle but for a different purpose, therefore you would say something like this:

Everything that I do, say, or think is governed by Divine Intelligence and inspired by Divine Wisdom. I am guided into right action. I am surrounded with friendship, love, and beauty. Enthusiastic joy, vitality, and inspiration are in everything I do. I am aware of my partnership with the Infinite.

SPIRITUAL TREATMENT

Every thought of not being wanted, of being afraid, of uncertainty and doubt is cast out of my mind. My memory goes back to God alone, in whom I live, move, and have my being. A complete sense of happiness, peace, and certainty floods me with light. I have confidence in myself because I have confidence in God. I am sure of myself because I am sure of God.

The Spirit within me knows the answer to any problem which confronts me. I know that the answer is here and now. It is within my own mind because God is right where I am. I now turn from the problem to the Spirit, accepting the answer. In calm confidence, in perfect trust, in abiding faith, and with complete peace I let go of the problem and receive the answer.

I know exactly what to do in every situation. Every idea necessary to successful living is brought to my attention. The doorway to ever-increasing opportunities for self-expression is open before me. I am continuously meeting new and larger experiences. Every day brings some greater good. Every day brings more blessing and greater self-expression. I am prospered in everything I do. There is no deferment, no delay, no obstruction or obstacle, nothing to impede the progress of right action.

I identify myself with abundance. I surrender all fear and doubt. I let go of all uncertainty. I know there is no confusion, no lack of confidence. I know that what is mine will claim me, know me, rush to me. The Presence of God is with me. The Mind of God is my mind. The Freedom of God is my freedom.

Today I bestow the essence of love upon everything. Everyone I meet shall be lovely to me. My soul meets the Soul of the Universe in everyone. This love is a healing power touching everything into wholeness. I am one with the rhythm of Life. There is nothing to be afraid of. There is nothing to be uncertain about. God is over all, in all, and through all. God is right where I am. I am at peace with the world in which I live. I am at home with the Divine Spirit in which I am immersed.

NOTE: When treating another, say: "This word is for him (or her)," then continue exactly as though you were treating yourself.

BIBLES OF THE WORLD

*Fragments from the spiritual history of the race revealing
the fundamental Unity of religious thought and experience.*

JUDAISM and CHRISTIANITY

In God I have put my trust. I will not be afraid what man can do unto me.

Fear thou not; for I am with thee; be not dismayed; for I am thy God.

He giveth power to the faint; and to them that have no might he increaseth strength. Even the youths shall faint and be weary, and the young men shall utterly fall. But they that wait upon the Lord shall renew their strength; they shall mount up with wings as eagles; they shall run, and not be weary, and they shall walk, and not faint.

ZOROASTRIANISM

Religion founded by Zoroaster

For the three excellent things be never slack, namely: good thoughts, good words, and good deeds; for the three abominable things be ever slack, namely: bad thoughts, bad words, and bad deeds.

I will pray unto thee for help, with many consecrations, with good consecrations of libations: — that we, abiding in thee, may long inhabit a good abode, full of all the riches that can be wished for.

HELLENISTIC THEOLOGY

Now 'thinking-manifest' deals with things made alone, for thinking manifest is nothing else than making . . . And as He thinketh all things manifest, He manifests through all things and in all, and most of all in whatsoever things He wills to manifest.

With Reason (Logos), not with hands, did the World-maker make the universal world; so that thou thus shouldst think of Him as everywhere and ever-being, the Author of all things, and One and Only, who by His Will all things hath created.

RAJA-YOGA PHILOSOPHY

Therefore it is clear that Ignorance can be removed only by Wisdom.

MOHAMMEDANISM

If God help you, none shall overcome you; but if He abandon you, who is he that shall help you when He is gone? In God, then, let the faithful trust.

We created man: and we know what his soul whispereth to him, and we are closer to him than his neck-vein.

LESSON 2

SELF CONTEMPLATION
The Spiritual Unity of Life and Ideas

A Message from Ernest Holmes

We hope you enjoyed your first lesson and that you have read it over carefully several times.

In this lesson please give special attention to the commentary titled A Science of Religion and a Religion of Science, *for in it you will learn that law governs everything in the spiritual and mental world just as it does in the physical, and that a combination of deep spiritual feeling added to a definite conscious knowledge of the Law of Mind in Action will always produce the best results.*

We are sure that you have started using the spiritual treatment included in the last lesson. We shall not repeat this, but shall rest assured that you do turn each week to the simple instructions and follow them carefully. It is only as you apply the practice outlined in these lessons that you will really come to understand its deep meaning and its practical application, and it is this application that we are all interested in, for theories are of no use unless they are used.

We trust that you are interested in the Bible interpretations based on Troward's Bible Mystery and Bible Meaning *and that you will realize that this is more than a Bible story. It is the story of every man's life. The* Great Mistake *referred to in this lesson is the mistake we all make and one that each must correct within himself. We must all come to see that there is but one* Final Power *in the Universe, which is God.*

SELF CONTEMPLATION
The Spiritual Unity of Life and Ideas

(textbook reference: pages 68-70)

That there is One Ultimate Reality back of all things is a conclusion we cannot avoid. It is self-evident that two ultimate powers in the universe would be impossible. For if these two powers were just alike they would be one and not two, and if they were different from each other, and each were infinite, they would cancel each other and nothing would be left.

It is perhaps hard for us to comprehend the real meaning of unity. But we do inwardly sense that unity is absolutely necessary to Infinite Being. That the Infinite, or the Life Principle, is One, all the deep spiritual thinkers of the ages have declared.

As a matter of fact it really is not difficult to see that Spirit must be One Perfect Unit. We know that all physical forms are made of one universal energy. This energy is undivided. It takes form but it is never divided against itself. Even while the form changes, the energy remains the same.

It is self-evident that the inner movement of Life upon Itself can be likened to a mental movement. Just as we must think before we can do anything, so thought must precede all action. This inner movement has been called the Word of God.

The starting point of creation is the Word of Spirit. If you turn to page 392, last paragraph, you will read: *In Universal Mind is contained the essence of everything that ever was, is, or shall be . . . Things exist in the Universal Mind as ideas. Ideas take form and become things in the concrete or the visible world.* This means that for every visible fact in the objective world there must be an invisible idea which is the cause of the fact. To understand how to properly create ideas is to understand how to experience those facts which we wish to experience.

SELF CONTEMPLATION

Fear and faith, success and failure, are tied up in our thinking, and all because we are some part of the Whole and partake of Its nature. One thing we must understand is that man is some part of the experience of God, since the Thought of God must be the cause of all that exists.

Our text states that since there are many things there must be many ideas. But these ideas do not interfere with each other. There is plenty of room in creation for all created objects, and since the Creative Principle which we use is infinite, no matter how much we use It or how many people use It, It will never be exhausted.

In the principle of mathematics we may all use the figure two as many times as we wish without exhausting it. So the Life Principle back of our thought is not depleted when we draw upon It. And as there is no limit to the possible combination of numbers, so we cannot conceive of any limit to the number of ideas that can exist in the Universe. This is what our text means when it speaks of an infinite variety of ideas.

We should be careful to realize that many different ideas can proceed from the One Mind without in any way confusing the One Mind, or without in any way producing a quality or a division in this One Mind. Just as we can think many thoughts without dividing the mind against itself, so the Mind of God projects many ideas without confusion.

One of the most important things to understand at the very beginning of our lessons is the unity of all life. On page 493, second paragraph, you will find these words: *There is one Body and one Spirit. The entire creation is this Body. . . . Within this one Body are all bodies; that is, within the one creation — which is the product of the One Spirit — are all bodies.*

If you will study page 493 I am sure it will be clear to you that we all live in One Mind and that this One Mind is manifesting through each of us in an individualized way. This concept of Unity is the mystical secret of the ages. It is the key to the spiritual wisdom and the teachings of Jesus.

It was because Jesus perfectly understood his union with life that he knew man to be one with God. Because of this he had power, for any man's word will have power in such degree as he is conscious of his unity with Spirit.

Turn to page 646 and read our definition of *The Word.* The secret of our use of spiritual mind power lies in our ability to sense the Mind of God and to realize that It is operating through us. This will give us a conviction that nothing else can, and it will give us a power equal to our conviction.

You will soon perceive that the more conscious you are that good is supreme over apparent evil, and the more completely convinced you are that you are immersed in this good and that this good is working through you, the more quickly and easily you can dissipate evil.

On page 413, paragraph 3, you will find this expression: *To practice the Presence of the Divine in others is to practice mental healing for it is a recognition of this Divine Presence which heals. All the words used in the process of healing are for the purpose of building up this realization.* Please note the definition of *Divine Principle* on page 586 in connection with this idea.

Next we come to a paragraph on page 69 which states that *the Word of God is also the Law of God.* This means that the creative word, whether we think of it as the Word of God or as the word of man, acts in accord with an exact and mathematical law.

It also says in this paragraph: *It is evident that First Cause must be Self-Existent.* "Self-Existent" is defined in our Glossary (page 632) as *living by virtue of its own being,* which means that it is necessary for us to suppose a Final Power in the Universe, or an Omnipotence. In other words, how could we explain anything unless we accepted the proposition that Life is, and that Life creates through the medium of Its own Being?

This conclusion is more far-reaching than it appears to be. For if we are dealing with a Power which actually makes things out of Itself by Itself becoming or taking the form of the thing that It makes, and if this Power is Spirit, then it follows that the Word of God is also the Law of God. The Word of God is a conscious act, and the Law of God is a mechanical reaction.

SELF CONTEMPLATION

It is necessary to understand as a basic principle in our science that there is both an engine and an engineer; that is, the universe is volitional and mechanical. *Volitional* means having the attributes of consciousness and choice and self-determination; and by *mechanical* we mean an arbitrary, mechanical, automatic reaction. Thus we see that man as spirit is a free moral agent, but the Law of Mind which reacts to this free agent is merely another kind of mechanical force.

The more you think about these things the more thoroughly convinced you will be that this must be true. Does not the gardener plant his seed consciously? We cannot believe that the soil has any choice in the matter but it is an intelligent creative medium and does produce a crop. God as Spirit must be Conscious Life. The Universe as Law must be mechanical reaction.

If you will turn to page 488, *How to Demonstrate Liberty,* you will see how this principle works. In the third paragraph are these words: *Do not will or try to compel things to happen. Things happen by an immutable law and you do not need to energize the Essence of Being.* The wisest man who ever lived said, *Ye shall know the truth, and the truth shall make you free.*

What a marvelous concept to realize that there is something which, when known, automatically becomes demonstrated. This is exactly what you must come to realize — that your word is law. It is not law because you will it to be; it is law because that is its nature. There is no coercion in the process. Realization is quite different from coercion, and conviction is more than an act of the will. Feeling was born millions of years before the intellect came into being.

Let us consider the meaning of the word *Volition* as defined at the bottom of page 69: *There is but one volitional factor in the Universe, and this is Spirit, or the Self-Knowing Mind.* Our Glossary defines *Volition* (page 645) as *the power of conscious choice.* Hence our text might read: There is but One Power in the Universe which has self-choice, and that is the Self-Knowing Mind.

No doubt you have already discovered in the study of psychology that the conscious mind alone may choose and have independent action; while the subconscious, which really is the Law obeying the will of the conscious mind, has no volition whatsoever. The Self-Knowing Mind alone can choose. That is why it says, under the General Summary, page 396, third paragraph: *Mind as Law is helpless without direction. It has nowhere to go and nothing to do of Itself. It must be directed or It will do nothing.*

Read also the second paragraph on page 397: *God as Conscious Mind is Spirit. God as Subjective Mind is Law.* The Universe is a dual unity consisting of an active and a passive Principle. The projective power of Spirit is the active Principle, conscious, volitional; the receptive and creative Law is the doer of the Will of Spirit. We are surrounded by both the Spirit and the Law.

As a matter of fact we are some part of both. But is it not a wonderful thing to conceive of ourselves as having access to an Infinite Law as well as to a Divine Wisdom? It would be well for us to listen to the Divine Wisdom, and by the inspiration and guidance we receive from It learn how to give conscious direction to the Law. The Law, being mechanical and having no choice of Its own, must obey the Will of the Spirit.

On page 70 it says that God did not make Law or Substance; they are coexistent and coeternal with God. They always existed; they are without beginning and without end. Law and Substance, like God, always were. I am sure this is easy to understand since we all must realize that there never could have been a time when two and two began to make four. In this way we can say that the principle of mathematics is coexistent and coeternal with the Spirit.

But our text says that God is always creating forms and that nothing is moved unless Intelligence moves it in accord with Law. This means that Mind is the final Actor; Intelligence alone is the Originating Creative Cause. Whether this Intelligence is in what we call man or what we call God, It is the same Intelligence, since all Intelligence must finally be One.

To teach this creative power of thought is the whole purpose of the Bible. The Bible starts with the assumption that God is Spirit or Absolute Intelligence; that God's thought is creative; that man is made out of God and is like God. It follows that man's thought is creative.

On page 448 under the heading, *The Purpose of the Science of Mind,* you will find an explanation of the spiritual world as being the cause of the material. It follows that everything that Spirit thinks must take form. In other words the forms of nature are the thoughts of God outlined. Infinite Mind has brought this physical world into being. Therefore our thought interprets the physical world, and decides what our relationship to it shall be. What innumerable forms there must be which we do not yet look upon "for now we see through a glass, darkly."

This brings us to the end of Chapter I of the Textbook, and I suggest that you read it again in the light of this explanation.

SUMMARY

It is impossible that there should be two creative powers in the universe, because if there were one would destroy the other. Since there is but One Power in the universe, all action takes place within It. All things are made of It by movement of thought, mind, or consciousness within Itself. This is the meaning of *In the beginning was the Word.*

The fundamental cause of everything is an idea. There are infinite varieties of ideas in the Divine Mind. We are in the Divine Mind, and these ideas operate through us at the level of our own belief. Many ideas and many personalities, however, do not contradict the fundamental idea of the One Unity. It is the Mind of God in everything that makes everything what it is. There is One Body, One Mind, and One Spirit. We individualize this One, each in a unique manner. It was the knowledge of this that was the secret of the power of Jesus.

Good is at the base of everything. The more we recognize this good the more it will respond to us and the more power our words will have. The Word of God is the Law of God, or the Law of Mind in Action.

We are free agents in this Principle, and the conscious mind alone chooses. All subconscious reaction is automatic, mathematical, and mechanical. The thinker chooses. The Law of Mind in Action has no volition of Its own; It must respond.

QUESTIONS

Brief answers to these questions should be written out by the student after studying this lesson, and the answers compared with those in the Appendix.

1. Give two principal reasons why we believe in One Infinite Reality or Power behind all creation.

2. How can we have the many manifestations or creations from the One Ultimate Reality? Is this not duality?

3. What are the chief characteristics of the Ultimate Reality and of the world of manifestation?

4. What is the law by which these manifestations or creations are brought into being? How can man use this law?

5. Is Ultimate Reality ever depleted by becoming form?

6. Is all thought creative?

7. If thought is creative why is it that some of our treatments are more effective than others?

8. What is meant by the saying that *God is the engine and the engineer?*

9. What do we mean by: (1) Conscious mind?   (2) Subjective mind?

10. Are the conscious and subjective minds two separate minds?

METAPHYSICAL INTERPRETATIONS OF THE BIBLE

based on

Thomas Troward's *Bible Mystery and Bible Meaning*

THE GREAT MISTAKE

In his comments on *The Fall,* Troward says that the story of Eden is an allegory which represents the Garden of the Soul. In this symbolic garden grew two trees, the Tree of the Knowledge of Good and Evil, and the Tree of Life.

The Tree of Life symbolizes the Divine Nature, referred to in the Upanishads: . . . *This is the ancient tree whose roots grow upward and whose branches grow downward, that is called Brahma . . . All worlds are contained in it and no one goes beyond.* It symbolizes the current of Divine Life flowing through man's nature which the allegory calls the Garden of the Soul.

Philo said, *The Tree of Life is that most general virtue . . . from which the particular virtues are derived.* His reference to the Tree of Life has the same meaning which Troward gives it when he says that the Tree of Life is that innermost perception of Spirit.

If in speaking of the Garden of the Soul, which the Bible calls the Garden of the Lord, one has reference to the Creative Principle of Mind both in nature and in man, then naturally we should recognize the fruit which grows in the Garden of the Soul as being the fruit of thoughts and ideas which man must plant and cultivate, and from which he must reap a harvest. The Garden then is a thing of consciousness.

The Tree of the Knowledge of Good and Evil represents the possibility of a dual experience which arises out of man's freedom of choice. For even though our nature is rooted in the Divine, the immutable Law of Cause and Effect brings into our experience those conditions which correspond to the use we make of life; otherwise we could not be free.

Troward draws our attention to the thought that the story of Adam and Eve in the Garden is not the tradition of some bygone age, but the symbolical representation of what we all are in our innermost being. Thus Adam and Eve do not represent two persons, but rather two principles in human nature.

It is interesting that Eve was tempted, and that Adam was cast out of the Garden of Eden because he shared with her in the sin of partaking of the forbidden fruit. It becomes necessary, then, to investigate the meaning of fruit. Here we find a rich symbolism. Fruit represents the results of action, whether they be good or bad. It represents the operation of the Karmic Law, which is the Law of Cause and Effect. Thus Jeremiah says, *I the Lord search the heart, I try the reins, even to give every man according to his ways, and according to the fruit of his doings.* The fruit of the Spirit is symbolic of the higher nature: . . . *the fruit of the Spirit is love, joy, peace, longsuffering, gentleness, goodness, faith, meekness, temperance: against such there is no law* (Galatians 5:22, 23).

In ancient symbology the fruit of the ground represented the physical nature, which must be transmuted into the fruit of the Spirit. The fruit of the Tree of the Knowledge of Good and Evil symbolizes the mixed experiences of the individual on the pathway of his evolution from lower to higher planes.

Let us inquire into the meaning of the word Adam. Adam is symbolic of the lower aspect of mind, which Philo called the intellect. The word Adam also had a higher meaning and was symbolic of the higher nature, the Archetypal Man. The Cabala says, *In reading the first and second chapters of Genesis, a distinction was made by the learned of the Israelites between the higher Adam, i.e., the Adam Quadmon or . . . ideal man, and the inferior Adam.* The higher Adam also symbolizes the Christ. Thus in Corinthians we are told: *The first man Adam was made a living soul; the last Adam was made a quickening Spirit . . . The first man is of the earth, earthy: the second man is the Lord from heaven.* It also tells us that we must put off the old man, which is the first Adam, and put on the New Man, the last Adam, which is Christ. The last Adam, the prototype of the celestial, is the Universal Christ incarnated in every soul, waiting the redemption from the Fall, that through transition may become redeemed and sit at the right hand of the Lord. Here *Lord* refers to the Law of Mind or the government of the Karmic Law through the just decisions of Divine Wisdom.

The Chaldeans, Hebrews, and several other religious groups of antiquity spoke

THE GREAT MISTAKE

of the first man as Adam, and also spoke of the other Adam, which in some of the ancient sayings is referred to as *the First Adam who extended from the earth to the firmament,* for it is said that he was created upon or above the earth. In this illustration the Divine Image, or the Heavenly Adam, precedes and transcends the Adam of the dust. This means that Christ rules the Adam nature.

It is the Adam of the dust who makes the Great Mistake. This is the first man, who is of the earth, earthy. But the Christ Adam, the Divine Image, lifts the lower Adam into salvation. Thus it is written: *For as in Adam all die, even so in Christ shall all be made alive.*

Let us now turn to the meaning of Eve. Eve refers to the emotional nature of the mind functioning in the lower aspects, referred to in Genesis as the Mother of Creation: *And Adam called his wife's name Eve; because she was the mother of all living.*

Troward tells us that Adam and Eve represent two principles existent within us, one which can be deceived, can make mistakes, and the other which is incapable of being deceived, yet is involved in the fall of the former. This represents the active and passive principles in all people, or what today we call the conscious and subjective faculties of the mind. Eve, or the receptive side of our nature, receives the argument of error, represented by the temptation of the serpent, and in her turn extends the fruit of duality to the intellect, or the self-conscious faculties, represented by Adam. If we were to modernize this story it would be quite correct to say that the subconscious, being a medium for the activity of thought but having no choice or will of its own, is liable to receive any suggestion, and once having received such suggestion, to act as though it were true. Hence the intellect itself becomes coerced. It is temporarily held captive.

Most of our reactions are subconscious; by far the largest portion of the mind is submerged. In our allegory there is a vast field of subjective reaction, represented by Eve; creative but not selective, not discriminating. Hence it is Eve who listens to the serpent, who eats of the fruit of the Tree of the Knowledge of Duality, and who, having eaten, seduces the husband. The intellect stands for the husband.

From a psychological viewpoint the subconscious controls the conscious. That which today we call the subconscious, in antiquity was sometimes referred to as the *great feminine illusion,* that part of our nature which can be fooled. This does not refer to some external force operating upon us but to some part of our own nature. Plotinus said, *The universal law under which the individual falls is not outside but within each.* Also, from the Talmud: *Not God but ye yourselves are the creators and supporters of — evils.* But because we are ignorant of our Divine nature and of the consequent power that accompanies it, we use this nature destructively rather than constructively. As the narrative states, we listen to the argument of the serpent.

Inquiring into the meaning and nature of the serpent we must again look into ancient symbolism. In ancient mythology the serpent was sometimes an emblem of good, while at other times it designated the subtlety of evil. From one of the ancient Papyri we have this saying: *Heaven was on earth . . . the good and evil serpents did not exist,* which means that prior to any manifestation there is no duality. Everything emanates from one fundamental Unity which must be the essence of Goodness, Truth, and Beauty. When this One Pure Essence passes through incarnation into individualized Spirit, It carries with It the limitless creative power of Its own consciousness. Thus, automatically, man becomes endowed with creative thought.

Troward tells us that this creative power of thought is perfectly unlimited in itself, but its action is limited by the particular conception which it is sent forth to embody. Ignorance of the Law excuses no one from Its results. If in ignorance we use the Life Principle destructively, our own creative thought-power externalizes conditions representative of our conceptions, and we become involved in a network of circumstances from which we can find no way of escape. The key to the whole situation lies in the realization that these circumstances are self-imposed rather than imposed on us through some external force, power, or intelligence.

We judge according to appearances. This is what Troward calls the Great Deception, and this is what ancient symbolism depicts as the serpent. The serpent argues that evil is equal to good; that there is a power separated from the living creative Spirit and opposed to It. Ancient literature also speaks of serpents which appear not only on earth but in the air and sky. In John 3:14 we find: *And as Moses lifted up the serpent in the wilderness, even so must the Son of man be lifted up.*

THE GREAT MISTAKE

We see, then, that the serpent is symbolized as both good and evil. Barlow, in his *Essays on Symbolism*, says, *The serpent has had a good meaning given to it and a very bad one. It has been the emblem of wisdom, and par excellence, the symbol of sin. With a pair of wings it became the Seraph. Curled up in a circle it has stood for time without end.*

The three-headed serpent symbolized the threefold nature of Reality, just as does the Christian Trinity. It was the Triad. It is evident, then, that the serpent symbolized the Life Principle Itself and the different viewpoints which one may take of It, together with the inevitable corresponding results. This is why Troward tells us that by thinking of evil as a thing in itself we give it the very power which we pray it may be robbed of. By the act of our creative thought, the evil which we experience is brought into existence.

Listening to the serpent may be construed as listening to what Troward calls secondary causes; judging according to appearances rather than righteously; judging from the viewpoint that there is more than One Causation, thus making evil equal to good.

The story of Adam and Eve, then, becomes the story of every individual's life. That part of his psychological nature which can be fooled, symbolized by Eve, receives the suggestion of separation, and through continuous repetition gradually coerces the intellect or the self-conscious faculties, represented by Adam, until the whole psychological man is brought under the influence of subjective thought patterns. It is generally considered that much, if not most, of our conscious actions are definitely influenced by this unconscious field of thought, which rising from the habit nature tends to control our actions.

This does not mean that evil is a thing in itself. And yet it is more than a belief. It is a solid conviction. In our science we learn to separate the evil from the one experiencing it, since evil itself is not person, place, or thing, and belongs to no one. The Talmud states: *Pray not that sinners may perish, but that the sin itself may disappear.*

The knowledge that good is supreme will automatically destroy evil. *By knowledge of God all bonds are destroyed. . . .* The Koran says, *I say: Truth is come and falsehood vanished. Verily falsehood is a thing that vanisheth.* From the Zend-Avesta: *The word of falsehood smites, but the Word of Truth shall smite it.* From the Gita: *I destroy the ignorance-born darkness by the shining lamp of wisdom.* And in II Corinthians: . . . *for what fellowship hath righteousness with unrighteousness? and what communion hath light with darkness?* Again, the Koran states: *Whatever good betideth thee is from God, and whatever betideth thee, if evil, is from thyself.*

Such passages might be endlessly quoted. It is sufficient to know that the deep spiritual thinkers of all time have realized that the problem of evil is not a problem concerning something that has power within itself. It deals with the creative power of our own thought. The argument of the serpent is any argument in our consciousness which denies the supremacy of good. For as Troward tells us, if God, or the Originating Creative Principle, is One, then any suppositional opposite to this One is zero.

It would be impossible for . . . *two principles to neutralize each other, one of which is, and one which is not.* We can never suppose that the great nothing is equal to the Great Something. And yet this is exactly what we often do when we judge according to appearances. For instance, we say that since poverty has always existed, it always must exist.

Now this is just where we make our mistake. We eat from the fruit of the Tree of the Knowledge of Good and Evil and it is really the Law of Liberty that permits us to do this. The fruit of the Tree of Life Itself is not evil, but merely a result of action. The Tree of Life which grows in the garden of our own soul is a tree which bears many types of fruit. All manifestations come from One Final Power. Our own Divine individuality differentiates this Power into innumerable experiences. If our thoughts are always received from the Great Reality and from the knowledge that the One is ever expressing Itself in many forms, then we shall come to see that It can as easily express beauty for us as ugliness. But if we have not yet learned how to see beauty instead of ugliness, then because thought is creative, ugliness appears in our experience. Hence the One Power appears to us as evil.

The evil, however, is merely a result of our own confused thought and is never a thing in itself. Hence we discover this paradox, that the very fear of evil creates its experience, while faith in good is enduring. The Truth always neutralizes fear and dissolves evil experience.

One of the most difficult things for us to learn is that each one individualizes the Spirit, and as such each is a law in his own life under the One Great Law of all life. Life becomes a mirror reflecting those conditions into our experience which mathematically correspond to our subjective attitudes of thought. In such degree as we come to see that God or Good is the only positive and absolute Power and Presence, and in such measure as we perceive this Divine Presence in our experience as Goodness, Truth, Beauty, Harmony, etc., in this measure we shall experience Reality, not as duality but as unity.

The idea in Genesis that if one eats from the fruit of the Tree of the Knowledge of Good and Evil he shall be as God and live forever, has a hidden but an interesting meaning, and one of utmost simplicity. It resolves itself into this: Man, a center of God Consciousness, gradually becoming aware of himself and of his relationship to the Universe, is on the pathway of experience, evolution, or unfoldment (whichever expression one chooses to use). His thought is creative, and because he has freedom of choice, that which he chooses, either through fear or faith, tends to become part of his experience.

Since evil and good are not two ultimate powers arrayed against each other, for evil is merely an inverted use of good, it follows that by experience we all shall learn to live constructively. Meanwhile we suffer the experience of a destructive use of the Law of Life — this is *The Fall. Redemption,* of course, means just the opposite. It means a complete salvation from everything designated by the Fall.

Troward concludes: *If then it were possible for him (man) to attain the knowledge which would enable him to live forever before gaining this experience, the result would be an immortality of misery.* This would be true because it would make evil equal in power with good. Hence there is a judgment pronounced against the serpent, which stands for the lower use of the Life Principle, until the day of salvation, that is, the elevation of the serpent, which then becomes the Savior. Serpent and Savior designate two possible uses of One Life Principle.

Troward summarizes his findings: *Thus the story of The Fall contains also the statement of the principle of the Rising-again.* So we come back to the old saying: *For as in Adam all die, even so in Christ shall all be made alive.* No more definite statement could be made than that man himself is both heaven and hell. While duality exists only in our imagination, our belief in it becomes an experience which is real enough while it lasts, but by lifting up *the serpent in the wilderness,* that is, by elevating the Life Principle in the midst of fear, pain, and impoverishment, we may look upon It and be made whole.

A SCIENCE OF RELIGION and A RELIGION OF SCIENCE

There are three channels through which knowledge comes to us, namely, science, philosophy, and religion. By *science* we mean an organized knowledge of natural law and its application to life. By *philosophy* we mean the opinions one holds about the world, life, and reality. Although we generally speak of philosophy in relation to those statements which have been put down in writing by men whose opinions we respect, as a matter of fact, philosophy is anybody's opinion about anything. By *religion* we mean any man's belief about his relation to the invisible Universe. Or we might say religion is a man's idea of God or gods.

It follows, then, that there are many philosophies and many religions, since in both instances they constitute opinions. But not so with science, for science is a knowledge of the laws of nature. We also speak of *pure science* and *applied science*. Pure science means the application of these natural principles to human needs. Thus pure science is a knowledge of principles, while applied science is a technique for using universal principles.

A scientist, in whatever field of investigation he may be engaged, is one who uses universal principles. Once a principle is discovered and the laws governing it are ascertained, he maintains absolute faith in that principle.

Science is not an investigation into the *why,* but into the *how.* The why of anything, that is, the reason for its being, the reason for Being Itself, science makes no attempt to answer. Should it shift its field from the knowledge of principles and facts to the field of inquiry into why these principles exist, then science would become philosophy.

Today scientific minds are beginning to speculate on their own principles. And as they do this their speculations fall into two generalized classifications, philosophically speaking. These speculations lead them either to a philosophic basis of *materialism* or to a philosophic basis of *idealism.* For all philosophy finally falls into these two branches of thought — idealism and materialism.

A SCIENCE OF RELIGION and A RELIGION OF SCIENCE

Both the idealist and the materialist believe that the universe is a thing of intelligence. The only difference is that the materialist refuses to admit that the intelligence operating through the laws of nature is backed by or permeated with any form of consciousness; that is, the intelligence is merely a blind but intelligent force, a conglomeration of immutable laws of cause and effect with no element of consciousness, no sentiment, no feeling. He sees only blind force, but he sees blind force intelligently organized.

The idealist feels that back of and operating in and through the laws of nature there is volition and consciousness, for he argues that the manifestation of physical life upon this planet always is in accord with organized intelligence. He argues that organized intelligence can be accounted for only on the basis that there is an engineer as well as an engine.

There are, then, these two branches of philosophy — the idealistic and the materialistic. The idealist believes in consciousness, hence an Oversoul or a Spiritual Universe, while the materialist does not. Naturally the scientist who is philosophically a materialist believes in no God, no spiritual universe, and no consciousness in the universe which responds to man. He does not believe in the immortality of the individual soul, nor can he give any real meaning to life. He may be a humanitarian and a very good man, but his ultimate philosophy is: "Six feet under and all is over."

The scientist who feels that there is consciousness in the universe finds no difficulty in believing in God or in the universe as a spiritual system, permeated with a consciousness which responds to man. Therefore he believes in prayer, faith, immortality, and a definite meaning to life. An increasing number of scientific men are taking this position. The scientist who is a materialist has no religion unless it be one of humanitarianism, while the idealist can scarcely get along without some religion.

But if the idealist is a scientific man, believing as he must that everything is governed by law, his religion cannot be superstitious. Being a scientific person he cannot believe in a God who specializes on one person more than on another, or who esteems one person above another, nor can he believe that the laws of nature can be broken or modified through anyone's prayer or faith. Therefore the scientific mind which happens at the same time to be idealistic, that is, believes that the universe is not only intelligent but that it is also consciousness, will be satisfied with no religion which contradicts reason, common sense, and a cosmos of law and order.

When the first discoveries of science refuted ancient superstitions and proved that this world was not the center of the universe, that it was round and not flat, the faith which many people held began to wane. The ancient shibboleths, dogmas, and superstitions could no longer be held valid for intelligent men. So they were discarded, and religion began to lose its hold on the scientific mind.

This marked but a certain stage in the evolution of science, for today we find increasing numbers of scientific men emerging from this age of materialism, particularly since science has now theoretically resolved the material universe into organized energy, and has discovered that the smallest particles which it supposes to exist exercise a sort of volition, which of course leaves room for freedom. Once you establish freedom and volition operating upon, in, or through the energy which creates form, then you have established a universe of consciousness. And once you establish a universe of consciousness you establish the possibility of communion, and arrive at a logical basis for faith, prayer, the religious and the mystical life.

During this mental and spiritual controversy which has taken place in the world in the last few hundred years, the vast majority of people have given but little thought to the subtle intricacies and the deep abstractions which we have been considering. To most people religion was either superstitiously entertained — and no doubt with great benefit to those who believed it — or else it was rejected.

Today, however, there is a certain and rather swift return to religious convictions. The reason for this appears to be twofold. It has been discovered that when all religious atmosphere disappears, when every mystical element is eliminated, and when man views the universe merely as blind force, he loses hope. He views life as an unfortunate experience and looks forward to death as a happy oblivion. No mental attitude could be designed which would create a more forlorn outlook than this.

Moreover, when the mass consciousness becomes irreligious, unmystical, unbelieving, and without faith in God, without any conviction as to the meaning of life, it becomes chaotic, anarchistic, irresponsible, and in effect says, "Eat, drink and be merry, for tomorrow we die." Therefore it again becomes necessary that some form of religion shall be given to the world which scientific men need not reject and which the unscientific man may accept without superstition.

This is exactly what we mean when we speak of a *scientific religion*. We do not mean that we reduce religion to coldness, without sentiment or feeling, but that we add law and order to the sentiment and the feeling. We have a perfect right to speak of a scientific religion or a religion of science. But upon what natural principle should a scientific religion be based? It must be based upon the principle of Mind, Intelligence, and Consciousness.

A scientific religion may still affirm Consciousness in the Universe, that is, a spiritual Presence and an Intelligence which respond to the individual approach. Therefore a scientific religion does not exclude what we call prayer or communion even though it lays greater stress on communion than on petition. For instance, a scientific religion does not believe that man's petitions to God can change the natural order of the universe or reverse the laws of nature.

It does believe, however, that prayer is the communion of the soul with the Oversoul or with God, which makes it possible for man, not to reverse natural law but to reverse his position in it in such a way that bondage becomes freedom.

We might speak of *pure Religious Science* as we would speak of a *pure natural science,* which means the study of natural causes. We might speak of pure Religious Science as that branch of science which studies the nature of the Divine Principle, the nature of Mind and Consciousness. Then we would think of *applied Religious Science* as the application of this Divine Principle to human needs for practical purposes, and this is where the Religious Scientist, in applying his Principle, would study the nature of prayer, of faith, and of mental actions and reactions.

He would discover that in using faith, prayer, communion, or what we call mental treatment, he would be applying the Principle of Mind, Spirit, Intelligence, Consciousness, Law and Order to the persistent problems of everyday life. He would, then, be more than a theoretical religionist; he would have an applied and a practical religion.

A SCIENCE OF RELIGION and A RELIGION OF SCIENCE

This is exactly what we mean when we speak of a science of religion and a religion of science, for we are using this term in its broadest sense. We are using the term *religion* from the standpoint of universal religion, including all religious beliefs — Christian, Buddhist, Mohammedan, or any other faith — and we are thinking of prayer, communion, and the laws of consciousness as applied to any and all people. In short, we are universalizing the Principle. Thus each religion approaches the same God, all religions ultimately believe in the same God, but a scientific religion cannot believe in any concept of God which denies a universe of Law and Order, or which attempts to exclude anyone from its benefits.

It would be unscientific as well as irrational to believe that God, or the Supreme Intelligence, holds one man in higher esteem than another. For as the Bible so truthfully and boldly declares: *And let him that is athirst come. And whosoever will, let him take the water of life freely.*

A Religious Scientist believes with Robert Browning that *all's love, yet all's law.* He believes in an impersonal Law as well as in a personal relationship to the Spirit. And he must believe that this Law exists for all, like the law of mathematics or any other natural law, but that this personal relationship is personified through each at the level of his consciousness, at the level of his comprehension of what God means to him. In a scientific religion, superstition and dogma find no place. They must be discarded.

Intelligence and reason must be the rule of thought, and God must be accessible to all on equal terms. The scientific man cannot believe in special revelations or in special dispensations of Providence. He does not believe that Joshua made the sun stand still nor that Moses parted the Red Sea. He believes that these are but symbols of spiritual power, probably intended to teach us that the Spirit in man is supreme over all apparent material resistance.

The scientific religionist cannot believe in miracles, but he does not deny the power of spiritual thought. He believes that the so-called miracles performed as a result of spiritual faith have been in accord with natural law and cosmic order. He believes that they should be reproduced at will. That which the illumined have experienced and that which men of great spiritual power have proved, the scientific religionist feels should be deliberately used in everyday life.

A SCIENCE OF RELIGION and A RELIGION OF SCIENCE

He believes there is a Principle governing all things. He feels that he understands the laws, or at least some of the laws, of this Principle; hence he feels that it is intensely sane as well as humanly practical to apply faith, consciousness, and spiritual conviction to the solution of human problems. This is what is meant by *spiritual mind healing.*

Spiritual mind healing is based on the belief or the theory, which we now consider to be proved, that there is a Principle of Intelligence in the universe which is not only creative, giving rise to objective form, but is immediately sensitive to our desires; being universal It is omnipresent, and being omnipresent It is not only where we are but It is what we are. The difference is in degree and not in essence. Hence the scientific religionist feels that he understands what Jesus meant when he said, *The words that I speak unto you I speak not of myself, but the Father, that dwelleth in me, he doeth the works.*

Just as all pure science, before it can be of any use to humanity must pass into applied science, so pure religion, before it can have a practical application, must pass into applied religion. And it is the application of religion to the solution of our problems which we speak of as *demonstrating* the Principle.

What, then, is the Principle of pure and applied Religious Science? The Principle of pure Religious Science is that there is an Absolute Intelligence in the universe — one, undivided, birthless, deathless, changeless Reality. Since no one made God and since God did not make Himself, that which was, is, and is to be, will remain.

That which is, according to our first axiom of truth which says that the Truth is all there is, means that there is nothing else beside It. Hence the entire manifestation of Life is an evolution or an unfoldment of form from that which is formless, primordial, and eternal. This intelligent Cause, this undifferentiated and undistributed God-Principle, one and complete within Itself, yet from which all action proceeds and in which all creation takes place, this original and originating One is the absolute Principle of Religious Science.

In the philosophy of Religious Science we rightly deduce that since man lives, and moves, and has his being in states of consciousness, that is, since man can think, he exists. Since he can proclaim, he must be, and since he is, he must be made out of that which is, by reason of the fact that you can get out of a bag only what is in it. It was this perception, we believe, which was back of what Jesus meant when he said, *He that hath seen me hath seen the Father.*

The philosophy of Religious Science, then, consists in the belief, the opinion, or the certainty that God as man, in man, is man, and that when man makes a proclamation it is still God proclaiming, but now at the level of man's consciousness. Therefore the cosmos is reflected in or manifested by or through the individual. You cannot say, "Why is man?" any more than you can say, "Why is God?" Intelligence exists and man interprets It. Therefore man is Its mouthpiece; man is a personification of the Infinite, governed by the same laws. But man is more than law; he is consciousness.

The application of this science of religion and this philosophy of its thought to our everyday problems is the practical end of Religious Science, just as there is a practical end to every other science. It is not enough merely to speculate or philosophize. It is certainly not enough to abstract our thought and announce an Infinite, for the Infinite can never mean more to us at any time than the use which we make of It, just as electricity can never mean more to us than the use we make of it. This is true of any and all principles of nature.

Religious Science rightly argues that if there is an Infinite Creative Intelligence which makes things out of Itself by Itself becoming the thing that It makes, and if man exists and is conscious, then the creative Genius of this Universal Mind is also the creative genius of Its individualization, which we call man.

From the propositions stated above intelligence cannot escape, correct induction and deduction cannot escape. Thus most of the great intellectual geniuses who have ever lived on this planet have proclaimed these truths, each in his own tongue, in his own language, in his own day, for his own age, and we believe that Jesus proclaimed them for all ages since he was so universal in his concept.

Religious Science does not belong to any sect, to any group, to any class, and most certainly not to any person. It lays no claim to special revelation, but does announce that in its particular system of thought there have been gathered together facts from all ages, from all people, from all philosophies and religions; and using the practical methods which any other scientific research would use it is able to, and does, deliver a message of freedom.

MEDITATION

Since God is Love, and God is All in All, Love must be the underlying Principle of life, and therefore in all. This Life is my life. This Love I am. It is the very essence of my being.

I know that Love is harmony and peace and joy. In it is all good, all that is true, all that is beautiful. It is perfect balance, perfect poise.

Love heals everything, every imperfection of mind or body or environment. Love overcomes hatred, anger, envy, criticism. Where Love is there is no room for any negative emotion. Love is the Great Adjuster.

I empty my mind and heart of all but Love. I let Love express in me, through me, and flow out into my world of thought and action. *I AM Love.*

I AM Love — that is harmony,
I AM Love — that is peace,
I AM Love — that is joy,
I AM Love — that is freedom,
I AM Love — that is wisdom,
I AM that Love that is in all.

I AM LOVE

LESSON 3

CREATIVE THOUGHT

MIND . . . The Greatest Discovery

A Message from Ernest Holmes

We take great pleasure in sending you Lesson 3 in the Principle and Practice of the Science of Mind. This lesson deals with mental laws and how they operate, and we should like to be certain that you are beginning to differentiate between the Law of Mind in Action as a mathematical principle, and the Living Spirit as a Divine Presence. We are surrounded by an intelligent Creative Principle which acts upon our thinking, and also by a Divine Presence which inspires this thinking. We commune with God but we use the Law.

These are the two foundations upon which this whole course is built. They are both simple and profound and have been taught by all of the deep thinkers of the ages.

As you will notice in our Supplement on the Bible, there is no danger in using the laws of nature or Laws of Mind when they are used constructively. We should be careful to use our thought for life-giving purposes only, and with the desire that we bless everything we touch. If we do this nothing but good can come to us.

Please note carefully the article The Use and Meaning of Words in Mental Treatment, *for this is of vital importance.*

Also examine the several pages from Bibles of the World, *and you will find that there is almost complete agreement among them, which shows that all great spiritual thinkers of the ages have agreed on fundamental truths. They have all communed with the same God, and received the same answer. We too must do this.*

CREATIVE THOUGHT

Mind . . . the Greatest Discovery

(textbook reference: pages 71-77)

Our lesson begins with the thought that nature waits on man's self-recognition. The laws of nature have always existed. Moses might have had electric lights instead of torches, but Moses did not know anything about electricity although electric energy filled the universe then as now. We might say that electricity waited on man's recognition of it and his conscious cooperation with the law governing it. Man did not have it to use until he first recognized its existence and understood how it worked.

This of course is true of every law of nature; any law that ever has been discovered by the scientific world must first have existed and in a sense waited to be used. All advance in science is a result of gaining more knowledge and a deeper understanding of the laws of nature and how they work. What untold possibilities lie before the scientific world only the imagination can depict. Everything happens as though the evolution of man were the result of a gradual awakening of his relationship to the universe and to the laws governing all life.

We do not believe that the Principle of Life has evolved; we cannot believe that God is more complete than He was a million years ago. What we do believe is that the manifestation of God is forever unfolding before us. As man's vision gradually increases, new laws and new conditions are revealed to him which in his former ignorance he neither believed in nor understood.

The laws of nature have always existed and the possibility of using them has always existed, for principles never change — what changes is the practice of principles. It is marvelous to consider the possibility of such an infinite and endless unfoldment. There must be beings as far in advance of us as we in our present

LESSON 3

state have evolved beyond the tadpole or the crocodile. Jesus said, *In my Father's house are many mansions*. There are many states of consciousness, many planes of self-expression. Man's being is founded on a limitless Principle; hence the evolution or unfoldment of his becoming — that is, of his manifestation — must also be without limit.

There will always be new worlds to conquer, the horizon of previous experiences will ever be rising over a new day. *Life waits on man's discovery of natural laws, his discovery of himself, and his discovery of his relationship to the great Whole* (top of page 72).

Next we have this thought: *The* principle *of any science is invisible*. On page 631 in the Glossary you will find *Science* defined as *knowledge of laws and principles; organized knowledge*. The principle of science is invisible. We do not see Life; we experience It. And because we experience It we know that we live. Life must forever remain invisible, yet what intelligent person would deny Its reality? (Read very carefully the definition of *Life*, page 606; and the whole paragraph on page 490, *The Ascending Scale of Life*.)

There is no end to our evolution, but the invisible Principle of Life we experience without seeing It. We can analyze how It works, but not what It is. You will readily see that in the last analysis we must accept Life rather than explain It. For instance, the united intelligence of the human race does not know how it is that we can eat lamb stew and apple pie and have it converted into whiskers and fingernails. We may watch the process, but the principle of that process we cannot see.

It is written: *No man hath seen God at any time; the only begotten Son, which is in the bosom of the Father, he hath declared him* (John 1:18). We do not see Causation; but the Son, which is the creation, does reflect or manifest or prove the existence of Causation. In this way God is revealed to us. Who is there who has ever seen love? Yet no one doubts its reality. (This is the meaning of the second paragraph on page 406, General Summary, in which we discuss the idea that Pure Spirit exists at the center of all form. We see the form but not the Spirit.)

Now turn to page 74 under the heading *Science*. One thing we must keep in mind is that God as Pure Spirit is an Infinite Presence, while the Universe as

CREATIVE THOUGHT

Law is mechanical. Science is the study of the mechanics of the Universe, just as religion is the study of real values and the relationship between God and man. Science, of necessity, must deal only with cold facts. There may be a sentiment in the mind of the scientist, but there cannot be any sentiment in his approach to Universal Principles. He discovers they are always exact, always mathematical, and always responsive to him, but they will never work for him until he has first discovered their nature and the mode of their response.

Is this not true in dealing with all the laws of life? We must first obey the laws of nature, then they will serve us. In the unfoldment of any science the laws governing that science must first be discovered, and then through careful, painstaking, and patient investigation, ways, methods, and means of using those laws are finally worked out.

The knowledge of law as principle is the foundation of any science; the knowledge of how this law works is the technique of that science. The science itself does not belong to anyone. It is always impersonal; it does not care who uses it. (Read the definition of *Impersonal* on page 601.) It is always neutral, it does not care for what purpose it is used; but it is always effective when we approach it in its own nature. The laws of science, being universal, belong to everyone. We might truly say that each possesses all the laws of nature. They are, in a sense, a personal belonging since each may use all of them, but since they are universal they are impersonal in that no person can ever exhaust them.

We rob no man when we seek our own good. Life exists for the purpose of self-expression — the more we express the more completely God is expressed. It does no one any good for us to remain poor, weak, sick, or unhappy. Rather we glorify God in such degree as we become emancipated from our bondage. I am sure we all believe this final emancipation can be attained only through the closest cooperation with the purpose of nature; only by a more complete sense of our unity with the Divine Spirit, which is the Infinite Presence of Life, Truth, Love, and Wisdom.

When it comes to the scientific use of any law, whether it is the science of electricity or the Science of Mind, let us forswear superstitions and approach it with intelligent understanding, for this is the only way we shall ever derive any benefit from our studies. As our text says in the second paragraph, page 75, *The Science of Mind, then, is the study of Life and the nature of the laws of thought.*

When we make the claim that there is a Universal Mind and a Universal Spirit we are announcing that there is a Principle back of all thought. We are announcing that the Spirit operating upon the mental Principle produces all forms. We are announcing the presence of a Divine Knower and the certainty of a mechanical response — the Law and the Word. (Turn to page 641 and carefully study the definition of *Universal Spirit.*)

We must be careful in this connection not to confuse the idea of the Spirit of God and the Law of God with any concept of duality. They are really two attributes of the same thing, just as seedtime and harvest are but two ends of one process of evolution. In the interpretation of Romans 12:2, referred to on page 486, under the heading *The Renewing of Your Mind,* you will find a discussion of the thought that mental healing is subject to the exact laws of Mind and Spirit and is accomplished by correct knowing. This knowing is a mental attitude toward the Truth. It is the Truth which makes us free and it is the mind which knows the Truth.

On page 407, second paragraph, is the statement: *We cannot account for the seen without having faith in the unseen.* Therefore in dealing with the Science of Mind as a study of life and the nature of the laws of thought, we must never forget that we are dealing with a definite Principle. We must learn how to deal with it consciously, knowing that as a result of our conscious thought there will be a subjective reaction in the Law which will exactly balance and equal that conscious thought.

The reaction of the Law is in the nature of a reflection of the image held in thought. Both the reflection in the mirror and the image in front of it are effects. Someone has placed the image in front of the mirror and the mirror must automatically reflect its exact likeness. The invisible cause of both the image and the reflection is the image maker. Here we have a perfect analogy of our use of mental law and of the mechanical reaction to our thought.

But again we must be careful not to confuse this with any system of duality. The mechanical reaction of the Law is a part of Being Itself and is in no way separated from It. Always we must be careful to avoid any confusion which arises from a belief in duality. (Read very carefully the definition of *Duality* on page 587, and the definition of *Unity* on page 640.)

When you say that there is a Universal Mind and someone asks you if you have ever seen It, be quite frank and say "No," and then ask him if he has ever seen Reason, Love, Integrity, or Beauty. Of course you have never seen the Universal Mind! Our text says (page 75), *The Eternal Principle is forever hidden,* and *The only proof we have of Mind is that we think.* We are undoubtedly living in the Universal Mind. Everything happens exactly as though we were living in a Universe of Pure Spirit from which we may receive intuitive perceptions and inspiration and Divine guidance.

At the same time, we are surrounded by a Universal Law of Mind which reacts creatively to our images of thought. From this standpoint you will better understand the statement on page 76 to the effect that what appears to be outside is really inside. That is, nothing is external to mind. Mind is both individual and Universal. (Read the explanation of *Mind* on page 612 and of *I Am* on page 598. Also study page 391 of the General Summary and the first three paragraphs of page 392.)

One of the most difficult things for us to understand, yet one which is absolutely essential, is the saying at the end of the second paragraph, page 76: *The Mind which is personified is the same Mind which is Universal.* Also read the thought at the bottom of the page, that the Intelligence which perceives nature is the same Intelligence that created it. Is not this really what Jesus meant when he said, *I and my Father are one?* In the first paragraph on page 77 you will notice these words: *God exists in me, and because God exists in me, I am able to recognize other beings in whom God exists.* We must never fail to realize that the Divine Creative Medium which is the Principle back of the movement of thought, is governed by the Divine Creative Presence which is the Spirit of God. And as we more and more completely sense the Divine Spirit as being our Spirit, we shall have an increasing power in our use of the Law.

SUMMARY

The Principle of Mind has not evolved. We are merely coming to understand how It works. All scientific research is in the realm of laws that pre-existed the human inquiry.

The laws of nature wait on our recognition but respond to us the moment we use them. This is true of the Law of Mind with which we are dealing. This will always be true because evolution is eternal.

There are limitless possibilities within the human being because he is not merely human, he is Divine. These possibilities wait for our recognition. This recognition is a spiritual act of the mind.

It is not strange that we do not see God, Spiritual Mind, or First Cause. Nor do we see mathematics, harmony, love, or beauty. All we see is the effect of these things. We have just as much reason to believe in the Universal Mind Principle that responds to us as we do in the law of gravitational force.

There is no sentiment in our approach to the Law of Mind, since it is mathematical, mechanical, and exact. The sentiment is in the way we use this Law. We must get it firmly established in our thought that there is a Principle of Mind and a science or a way to use It.

This science does not belong to any individual but it belongs to whoever uses it.

We have no superstition about this any more than a mechanic is superstitious about his engine. We are the mechanic using the engine, or the force and energy of a Creative Intelligence. We have access to this whole Creative Intelligence, even as each one of us has access to the whole of God.

QUESTIONS

Brief answers to these questions should be written out by the student after studying this lesson, and the answers compared with those in the Appendix.

1. What is the basic truth about any law of nature?

2. When can we use the laws of nature?

3. Does the Principle of Life or God evolve?

4. Does the Creative Spirit make something out of nothing?

5. Will man ever reach the apex of his evolution?

6. How does man progress?

7. Do we see natural causes, principles, or spiritual realities?

8. (a) Can we explain life?   (b) How then is God revealed to us?

9. What main idea should we keep in mind in studying this science?

10. How do we utilize the laws of nature?

11. To whom do the laws of nature belong?

12. What is the purpose of life?

13. How do we glorify God?

14. How can final emancipation from bondage be accomplished?

QUESTIONS

15. What is the Science of Mind?

16. What do we mean by the Law and the Word?

17. How is mental healing accomplished?

18. Does the idea of Spirit as Knower and Law as Doer imply duality?

19. What is the result of conscious thought?

20. Has anyone ever seen the Universal Mind?

21. Is man's mind separate from the Universal Mind?

22. How should we increase our use of Creative Mind?

METAPHYSICAL INTERPRETATIONS OF THE BIBLE

based on

Thomas Troward's *Bible Mystery and Bible Meaning*

GOD POWER AND THE NEW NAME

In his chapter on Israel, Troward explains the necessity of bringing all psychic forces under control. He says, *The psychic world is an integral part of the universe.*

This psychic world is frequently referred to in the Bible as water. As already stated, the story of the flood or deluge is symbolic of what might happen when the psychic life controls an individual or the race. Troward says . . . *a deluge would indicate a total submergence in a psychic environment which had become too powerful to be held under control.* Psychologically, in the case of an individual, this would happen when subjective thought patterns actually take possession of him and obsess him, creating a psychic confusion so complete that there is no longer a true integration of personality. Some form of insanity would follow such a condition.

If we can conceive of a world psyche, or what some psychologists might call a collective unconscious which largely dominates the race thought and action, we shall see that limitless confusion in this field would produce something akin to race insanity.

But the deluge referred to in the Bible, according to Troward, is attributed to the wickedness of mankind. Nearly all scriptures of antiquity refer to some form of deluge; that is, to some universal confusion which follows the misuse of the law of cause and effect, the law of causation and interaction between the higher and the lower plane. It is the law which says that we shall reap as we have sown. Hafiz says, *Do not complain, Oh soul! of the injustice of the Beloved, for such is thy law.*

All books of spiritual wisdom, particularly those of antiquity, warn us against a misuse of the Creative Principle. Most of them had some fictitious personage who, like Noah, outrode the turbulent waters of confusion. The ark symbolizes the preservation of Divine individuality even while the lower manifestations of life are swept away. In the *Ark of the Covenant* were kept the books of the law, symbolizing that in the Secret Place of the Most High, in the Christ within us, there is always a spiritual equilibrium.

It does not seem at all strange that universal belief should sway the opinions and acts of the human race, since we know that individual opinions do control to a large degree the actions of an individual.

Consider the reaction in what we call mob psychology. Its fear, hysteria, or heroism, something greater than any individual member, seizes all members. Or we may consider the act of collective faith beneficently healing, bringing peace, etc. This would be Christ walking over the waters — the Ark riding on the waters. The Spiritual Principle walks over, transcends, is above all psychic confusion, ever speaking from the depths of Its mystical Self: *It is I, be not afraid.*

This has been referred to as the movement of the Spirit upon the waters. It is from this movement that the psychic forces are brought under control and made to serve a good purpose. Troward is careful to point out that while there are certain dangers which might arise out of the psychic life, we must not fall under the illusion of either doubting its reality or refusing to have anything to do with it, for by our nature we are always immersed in it.

Common sense tells us that since this psychic realm is the realm of thought actions and reactions, the Law of Cause and Effect, it is impossible to escape it. We should use it as a servant rather than obey it as though it were a lord. And in order to do this both intelligently and constructively we must first recognize the Divine Principle of our being as one undivided, harmonious Goodness in which there is no violence whatsoever.

Just as there is no danger in using laws of nature unless they are used either in ignorance or with vicious intention, so no possible harm can come from the use of psychic powers, which are laws of mind, unless they are used either in ignorance or with vicious intention. Fortunately, ignorance soon destroys itself and vicious intention defeats its own purpose. The Universe must be foolproof in order to endure. Troward states that we are always safe when we recognize the Divine Spirit as the only source of power. This he implies is brought about by learning to see God in all things. For it is certain that we must accept life as either good or evil.

GOD POWER AND THE NEW NAME

Perhaps the greatest single mystery in life is the simple fact that life must become to each one of us what we are to it. The Law of Cause and Effect is no respecter of persons. We are at all times surrounded by a Creative Principle which accepts the images of our thoughts and acts creatively upon them. Consequently everything depends on the source from which we derive our thought patterns.

Are we controlled by the suggestion of our external environment? Do we judge according to appearances? If so we cannot hope to escape the limitations which now appear to hold us in their grasp. Suppose we are not controlled entirely by things as they appear objectively but that we are controlled by traditional beliefs which tend to limit us. If we are controlled from this subjective field our reflection in the Law of Cause and Effect is still limited to previous experiences. Whether we are bound by our psychic insight or our physical outsight makes no difference, for each furnishes us with images of limitation.

The Law of Mind like other laws in nature has to be used. But since it happens to be the greatest creative force we shall ever contact and since it is absolutely receptive to our thought, everything depends upon what our thought patterns are like and where they come from. Do they come from a belief that the highest Truth can be reached on only the lower physical or even the lower mental plane? If so we are building our Tower of Babel.

As Troward points out, this tower was built of brick, symbolic of the supposition that the external world is a thing in itself. This naturally leads to confusion, and as our text suggests, is the very opposite of the heavenly Jerusalem which is built of gold and precious stones. Gold is a symbol of spiritual qualities, Divine Wisdom, heavenly treasures — . . . *and the city was pure gold, like unto clear glass* (Revelation 21:18). Swedenborg tells us that frankincense represents spiritual goodness, and myrrh natural goodness. It is when this gold is joined with frankincense and myrrh that we have the true offering to life.

Here again we arrive at the trinity in unity. It is this recognition of the threefold unity of life with all of its implications that the wise men, the Magi, bring from the East to lay before the Babe in the manger at Bethlehem. The Magi came from the mystical East which symbolizes the source of heavenly light. They were guided by the Star. This star is the intuition which Wordsworth called our life's star.

It guides us across the pathway of human experience to where the little child lies in the manger of our innermost self. Manger is a symbol of spiritual simplicity and unity with all forms of life.

We also have the story of Moses who was found floating in a little ark. Coupling the mystical meaning of Moses, which Swedenborg tells us represents the Law, we find the symbol is that of the Law of Righteousness riding upon the waters of Mind. This stands for Divine Government. In the case of Jesus we find the Waters governed not only by Law but also by Love. St. John tells us that the Law was given by Moses, but that grace and truth came through Jesus Christ.

Returning to our story of the deluge and the Tower of Babel we find that the whole symbolism represents the operation of natural law directed by a state of confusion which is the result of a sense of disunity with the Creative Principle. The story implies that the more we know of natural law the worse off we are unless our knowledge is controlled by Divine Wisdom. Nothing could more perfectly describe conditions as they exist in the world today. Knowledge may be power but power without wisdom is confusion; hence the deluge.

Troward points out that the story of the Bible up to this point is an allegory. It is a symbolic word presentation describing the nature of man and the creative power of thought, and telling us what happens as a result of our thought. Troward tells us: *The purpose of the Bible is to convey instruction in the nature and use of . . . principles to those in whose hands this knowledge would be safe and useful.* These principles are few in number but they run through everything. The Bible repeats these few simple principles in innumerable ways, and is ever seeking to instruct the individual to awake to his own sonship.

Next we come to an explanation of the meaning of Jacob wrestling with the angel. Jacob is a symbol of the natural man trying to discover his relationship with the nameless One. Jacob's ladder represents the soul's path from the lower to the higher planes; from earth to heaven. Earth and heaven represent two states of consciousness. We are told that Christ has united heaven with earth.

The nameless One that Jacob wrestled was the great problem of his own relation to the Universal Spirit. He wrestled until the day broke, meaning until the light of Truth dawned upon his consciousness. This light is represented in Egyptian mythology by Ra, the ever-living Principle, symbol of the Higher Self of man and of the Supreme Self, which is God or Spirit. The Supreme Self manifests Itself as the Indwelling Self, which is called Khepera or the Indwelling Christ.

The new name which Jacob received, Troward tells us, signifies man's relationship to the universe of Spirit, soul, and body; the Spiritual, psychical, and physical. The new name is received in such degree as we become consciously aware of the Spiritual, the mental, and the physical. Our text states that it is only in the combination of all three elements that the true Reality is to be found.

Jesus said that we do not live by bread alone, but by every word that proceedeth out of Reality. He did not deny the physical universe, but told us not to judge everything by it. That is, to judge not according to appearances but to judge righteously. It is this righteous judgment which is designated by the word *Israel,* which means a knowledge of the truth of our being.

Troward said that Abraham, Isaac, and Jacob represent the three great Principles of Life; that which we in the Science of Mind often refer to as *The Thing Itself, The Way It Works,* and *What It Does.* The Universe is made up of Spirit, Soul, and Body. Spirit is the active Principle of self-assertion. Soul is the neutral, plastic, Creative Principle which receives the ideas of the active Principle and gives birth to form. Body is the physical universe or the universe of manifestation. It is the logical, inevitable, and mathematical result of the interaction of Spirit upon Soul.

Man also is spirit, soul, and body, thus partaking of the Divine Nature in each part of Its threefold aspects of cause, medium, and effect. In his evolution man awakes first to only the physical, and believes that he is entirely controlled by his objective surroundings. This is the period which has been referred to as tooth and claw, the survival of the fittest.

If at this point he fails to become aware of spiritual and unifying principles such as love, truth, beauty, and harmony, his awakening to the mental plane as a medium of power produces a confusion even greater than that which existed before he recognized the mental plane. Hence beside awakening from the material to the mental, there must be another awakening — an awakening of the mental to the spiritual.

When the spiritual animates the mental, the mental gives birth to that which is true. Consider this interesting quotation from Hermes: *All things accordingly that are on earth . . . are not the truth; they are copies of the Truth. Whenever the appearance doth receive the influx from above it turns into a copy of the Truth; without its energizing from above, it is false.* The Talmud says, *Unhappy is he who mistakes the branch for the tree, the shadow for the substance.* From the Gita: *The unreal hath no being (i.e. no being in itself), the Real never ceaseth to be.*

One could find innumerable sayings from the scriptures of many races descriptive of the transitory nature of the world of experience and the abiding nature of the Truth which governs it. It is not that we should deny the objective world, but rather that spiritual wisdom should inspire us to control it in accord with the laws of harmony.

From the creative power of our thought we can never escape. It is certain that we can neither change nor alter the laws of the universe. Within these laws there is perfect freedom, complete liberty, everlasting happiness, and eternal life. More we could not ask, greater could not be given. The universe, however, is always true to its own nature. We may trust in its integrity; we may rely upon its immutable laws whether we call them physical or metaphysical; and we may be certain that there is one underlying unity governing everything.

If there is any limitation imposed upon man it is only the limitation that the very nature of Reality automatically must impose, which is that we cannot use causation destructively without suffering. This is the whole meaning of sin, mistake, hell, and punishment. Spiritual Power is delivered on its own terms, and these terms are Unity, Goodness, Love, Justice, Truth, Beauty, etc.

It is not as though there were some deific power waiting for us to bow before its omnipotence, but that real omnipotence cannot be delivered while we use the power derived from it to destroy such omnipotence. We must never mistake liberty for license. God Power is delivered only when It is used in a Godlike way; but this is no restriction. There is nothing in the universe which denies us the right to use the highest Law to promote health, happiness, and success for ourselves and for others, provided our use of the Principle of Truth is constructive. It would be impossible to ask for more; it would be impossible for more to be given.

But how should we receive this great Good which has been given? As Troward has suggested, there is only one way that Power can be loosed through us, and that is through the creative act of our own consciousness. We must accept the Universe as Good or as evil; it will be to us a thing of limitation or of freedom. If our images of thought are generated by personal ambition, disregarding the greater good for all, then we shall be caught in a confusion of thinking.

The God Power which all potentially have can be used to the fullest extent only in a constructive way. Real Power, God Power, is Spiritual. Does this mean that the Spiritual contradicts either the mental or the physical? Not at all. The very word *Spiritual* implies a constructive use of physical and mental powers, and not some separate state of existence.

It is written that to be spiritually minded is life and peace, which means that we are both strong and peaceful when our thought processes are based upon a perception of the Unity of Good. But we are not consciously unified with Good while we desire to use Good for evil purposes. Hence it is written: *Thou shalt have no other gods before me.* That is, our faith should transcend all fear.

Are we daily watching our thought processes, being certain that all negative reactions are transmuted into positive acceptances? Do we really believe that Good is the final and only Power; that Love not only overcomes hate but completely annihilates it even as light converts darkness? These are the questions which daily we should ask ourselves.

We should be certain that our consciousness is continuously being enlarged. The whole purpose of life is to express the Self without fear or hurt to the Self or to anyone else. The gift of Life is made. We now know how to use it. No one else can decide for us but ourselves.

THE USE AND MEANING OF WORDS
IN MENTAL TREATMENT

The entire basis for spiritual mind healing lies in the assumption that we are now living in a Spiritual and Mental Universe; that Law is Mind in Action; that thinking and action are the same. And if thinking and action equal the same thing, certain kinds of thinking must constitute certain kinds of action. It logically follows that if one kind of thought produces a certain effect, then an opposite thought must produce an opposite effect.

Mental treatment is Mind in Action. A person should use those words which convey a meaning to his own thought. For instance, if he says, "This word is the law of elimination," he must feel that any condition which does not belong is actually being eliminated.

Since it would be impossible for him to believe that Mind could operate upon some matter or substance which is unlike Mind, he must first have resolved things into thoughts. For the practitioner does not treat a body separate from consciousness; he treats consciousness alone. Hence the state of inaction which he seeks to remove, so far as mental treatment is concerned, is neither a state of material nor physical inaction; for he has reduced the whole process to a state of mental inaction. It is evident that unless he could do this he could not give an effective mental treatment.

Thought alone can reverse thought, thought alone can handle thought, and only thought can demonstrate over that which is a result of thought. Therefore the mental practitioner theoretically resolves everything into Mind and proceeds upon the basis that Mind is form, or takes form, and that the form which it takes is still Mind. Our work is done in the realm of Mind alone. The words that we use should be simple, direct, and to the point, and should signify a meaning to our own consciousness.

The process of reasoning in treatment must be one which establishes man upon a spiritual basis, enthrones him in a Kingdom of Good, and gives him dominion

THE USE AND MEANING OF WORDS IN MENTAL TREATMENT

over all apparent evil.

If you say four and four make eight and eight has a meaning because you have already experienced handling eight marbles or eight oranges or eight chairs, then when you say four and four make eight you understand what those words mean. But do you understand what saying four million and four million means, even while your intellect announces eight million to be the answer?

Words must have value to the inner comprehension. I am sure Jesus understood this when he spoke of his word as being Spirit and Life. He spoke of his words as though they were entities. The thought and the thing cannot be separated. *The words that I speak unto you, they are spirit, and they are life,* implies that the words possess not only power but almost a degree of personalness.

In mathematics a person can correctly use his principle only as far as his understanding goes. This is also true in mental treatment. What is this understanding which he must have and which he must pour into the words which he speaks? He must understand his relationship to Being Itself, to God, to the Universe, and to Reality. There must be an interior awareness, a realization that Good is all the Power there is.

A practitioner uses words which imply to his own imagination the idea of movement, of explanation, of action or reaction, or whatever the desire is. That is, when he uses the word *elimination* he must know that something is being eliminated. He must have unqualified faith that there is a movement toward the desired elimination simultaneous with the word he uses. The practitioner must come to realize that thoughts and things are not separated; they are identical.

If he says, "Substance is supply and supply is money," and if he desires to demonstrate money, when he uses the word *substance* he should feel the presence of substance. Otherwise he is merely using a lot of words which have no meaning.

Surely we cannot separate thoughts from things in our treatment and hope to demonstrate things through thinking. For unless thoughts were things, then thoughts could not change what we call *things.* Indeed they would have no power over them whatsoever. It is upon this proposition that our whole science is based.

THE USE AND MEANING OF WORDS IN MENTAL TREATMENT

Since thoughts are things, different kinds of thoughts are different kinds of things. When the practitioner uses the idea of substance and supply in his imagination, the idea should not be divorced from the actual presence of whatever he thinks supply is, or whatever supply means to him.

Suppose he were conceiving the idea of *home*. It would not be enough for him to say, "I'm but a stranger here, heaven is my home." In this world *home* means house, tent, a place of residence, a place to live. Therefore if he wishes to demonstrate a home, when he uses the idea *home* there should be some corresponding reaction to the word which means the actual presence of a right place in which to live.

What words we can really use with spiritual meaning, significance, and reality, constitutes the stage of consciousness we are entertaining at any particular time. As a matter of fact our state of consciousness is what we are, and if we happen to be in business and wish to treat for right action we must realize that right action means being busy in the thing that we are doing. Business is the activity of consciousness, and the business of Mind is never inactive. Nor is the business of Mind limited to two, four, six, eight, ten, twelve, etc. It is as limitless as is our concept of it. Spirit is Good, therefore business is good, and we should know that our business represents our oneness with supply, with the Creative Cause, with the Creative Givingness, with the limitless activity of the Creator.

Our business enterprise is the demand which we make upon supply, and since the demand is answered, and can be answered only in terms of the demand made, and since there is no gap between, because both supply and demand are mental or spiritual, then it follows that supply follows demand, while demand does not limit supply but measures it out at the level of the demand made.

One man working for success might have the idea of enough money with which to pay the rent; another might have the idea that after the rent was paid he would have a few dollars left over; while still another might have the idea that paying the rent was merely attending to a detail and that out of the limitless abundance he should have money left which he could share with others.

There must be some reason why some succeed and others fail if the Universe in which we live is Intelligent. It is impossible to conceive of Mind as ever being unexpressed, and wealth and poverty are expressions of Mind, fulfilling an idea. The thought of success will create success. Mind thinks and it is done. Man's business is God's business and God's business is man's business, and there is only one business, which is the business of Life. Life is never inactive, never inadequate; it is always perfect, and your consciousness of right action is perfect. Your word is perfect and the thing to which the word gives form is perfect, and abundance is the only law there is — but your words must have meaning and their meaning is their power.

If you are treating to heal a physical disease, you should realize that material appearance is a mental formation rather than a law unto itself. Your realization that this formation is not necessary, and the significance of the statements which you make in declaring that your word is the law of elimination of the condition, should have the same reaction in your own thought as that which would be produced if, while you were looking at something, it should disappear. You would immediately recognize the omnipresence and the omnipotence of God, and to such degree as your recognition of the omnipresence of Good signifies to your own thought the annihilation of the negative physical condition, the condition will cease to be.

When the practitioner says, "This word is for so and so" or "for such and such a purpose," his definite intention specifies the place or the purpose, and this is all he needs to do. From then on his work is within himself, and his work is a combination of thinking, which through argument or realization brings about a complete acceptance of the desired fact. It would be impossible to do this unless facts could be reduced to states of consciousness.

That which needs to be externally changed is not a thing in itself but a physical state of consciousness. This is the crux of the whole matter; it is the finest of all points in metaphysical practice; it is the essence of the subject, but unfortunately it is too often overlooked. The external condition is not a thing but thought externalized, and thought externalized is still thought. A mental conclusion objectified is still a mental conclusion.

This is the meaning of argument in giving mental treatments. The argument is for the purpose of convincing the mind of the practitioner that the condition which needs to be changed is not a thing in itself; that back of it is a perfect Universe, God, the All-Being. But unless the words used by the practitioner in such argument have a definite meaning to him, implying life and action, they will have no power.

If we can understand that objective nature is a thing of thought, a Divine language, still plastic in the imagination of its conceiver, we shall know how to liken the laws of nature to the laws of thought, for this a metaphysician must do.

His work is specific in that it meets and repudiates a claim where the claim is — it denies it where it is and affirms the opposite — for he must meet the false argument either with an argument that is directly opposite to it, or by a realization which denies the argument without controversy. This is called *spiritual realization*. Therefore the condition must be met as though it were the surface form of a mental argument or state of consciousness, a suggestion rather than a thing itself.

GETTING AND GIVING

One of the laws of radiation says that the absorbing power of a substance is equal to its emitting power, which means that the ones that absorb the most must be the ones which emit the most. Or to state the proposition in another way, we can take in only what we give out. Jesus said, *Give, and it shall be given unto you.*

Now here is a law in nature verified by science, and we believe that every law in physical nature is reproduced in the Laws of Mind. This would have to be so if the Universe is one system rather than two, and if Unity is to be maintained throughout the whole.

There is a reason for these things, and the reason is that everything moves in a circle. Everything bends back upon itself. As a man sows so shall he reap, and so must he reap until he sows differently. Whitman said that the gift is most to the giver and comes back most to him, and we all know that since the universe is in balance nothing can leave any point without an equal something returning to it.

Each one of us is a point in the Infinite Mind, a center in the Consciousness of God or the Living Spirit. We do not live because we understand Life or even put Life into our own living; we live because Life lives in us. We could make no greater mistake than to think that we created either Life or Law, but it would be an equal error to suppose that we escape Life or Law. We are subject to it but not in any predetermined sense, for no matter what happened yesterday we can change its sequence today.

If we have given out but little and received only an equal amount, we can begin to give out more, and just as surely as we do this, more will return to us. The giving and receiving are at the center of our own being; going out from us is but one end of the coming back to us, and the coming back to us is merely the other end of the going out from us.

The whole thing is so simple that its very simplicity eludes us, and we look for a more profound reason for the universe being in balance, and why being in balance it automatically proclaims the law of justice.

If the going out and coming back are equal, then in a certain sense, like the energy and mass of Einstein, they are equal, identical, and interchangeable. To refuse to give is to refuse to live to the fullest extent. To refuse to give love is to refuse to receive love. That which we refuse to give out not only closes the door on the giving but on the receiving as well.

All this sounds like quite a tough proposition until we come to realize that if it were any other way we would not be free, but would be bound by external circumstances. Freedom can exist only on the proposition that it is first of all individual.

If we know that we ourselves are centers of distribution and centers of accumulation and that the two are equally identical and interchangeable, and if we know that nothing interferes with this but ourselves, we are free to act as we would be acted upon. This is why Jesus said, . . . *all things whatsoever ye would that men should do to you, do ye even so to them: for this is the law and the prophets.*

BIBLES OF THE WORLD

*Fragments from the spiritual history of the race revealing
the fundamental Unity of religious thought and experience.*

RAJA YOGA PHILOSOPHY

This manifested spiritual consciousness begins to manifest like the dawn in the pure heart, and shining like the midday sun in the *cave of wisdom* . . . illumines the whole universe.

The origin of pain can thus be traced to ignorance and it will not cease until ignorance is entirely dispelled, which will be only when the identity of the Self with the Universal Spirit is fully realized.

JUDAISM and CHRISTIANITY

He brought them out of darkness and the shadow of death, and brake their bands in sunder.

Unto the upright there ariseth light in the darkness.

For what fellowship hath righteousness with unrighteousness? And what communion hath light with darkness? And the light shineth in darkness; and the darkness comprehended it not.

The Lord is nigh unto them who are of a broken heart, and saveth such as be of a contrite spirit. Many are the afflictions of the righteous; but the Lord delivereth him out of them all.

In returning and rest shall ye be saved. In quietness and in confidence shall be your strength.

HELLENISTIC THEOSOPHY

Matter, my son, is separate from God, in order that thou mayst attribute unto it the quality of space. But what thing, else than mass thinkest thou it is, if it is not energized? Whereas, if it be energized, by whom is it made so? For energies, we said, are parts of God.

Then in this way know God; as having all things in Himself as thoughts, the whole Cosmos itself.

TAOISM

He has attained who knows what God is and who knows what man is. Knowing what God is, he knows that he himself proceeded therefrom. Knowing what man is, he rests in the knowledge of the known, waiting for the knowledge of the unknown.

BUDDHISM

Better one day of insight into the deathless state than a hundred years of blindness to this immortality.

Creatures follow the destiny of their deeds.

BIBLES OF THE WORLD

By the complete destruction of lust, hatred and delusion, devout men are no longer liable to suffering, and are assured of final salvation.

If a religionist desires to be assured of final salvation, let him be devoted to quietness of heart which springs from within; let him not drive back the ecstasy of contemplation; let him look through things.

JAINISM

Freedom from bonds is in your innermost heart. Knowledge, faith and right conduct are the true causes of final liberation.

CONFUCIANISM

The noble man is calm and serene. The inferior man is continually worried and anxious.

The noble man seeks what he wants in himself. The inferior man seeks it from others.

A wise and good man is occupied in the search for truth, not in seeking for a mere living.

A wise man should be solicitous about truth, not anxious about poverty.

HINDUISM

The wise should work desiring to promote the general good.

A wise man should always share with others.

Good words, good deeds and beautiful expressions a wise man ever culls from every quarter, even as a gleaner gathers ears of corn.

SIKHISM

All wealth is obtained by the love of God.

God's design cannot be set aside.

In whose heart the name abideth not — he it is who is poor.

LESSON 4

WORD AND LAW

Your Personal Word and the Impersonal Law

A Message from Ernest Holmes

May we draw your attention to the Supplement to this lesson, Desire, Opinion, and Revelation, *because we want you to think this over very carefully and come to realize the vast difference between unconscious desires, conscious opinions, and true spiritual revelation.*

Our lesson says that the Spirit is changeless and will never reveal one thing to one person and something else which contradicts this to another. Therefore you must always be careful to discriminate between truth and illusion.

We want you to become a scientific practitioner, which means that we want you to know how to use the Power that is within you to help and bless yourself and others; how to use It definitely for specific purposes. We want to be certain that you actually do it.

Again may we remind you to follow the instructions in Lesson 1 on how to give a treatment, and we certainly hope that you are doing this every day. There is nothing to wait for. The Law of Good already is around you, and your word that uses this Law already is in your own mouth. You are going to find that using this word is the most interesting experiment of your life.

May you be blessed in this endeavor.

PERSONAL WORD
AND
IMPERSONAL LAW

(textbook reference: pages 77-83)

In the study of mental laws we are considering one of the most vital, single points in our whole series of lessons. Your ability to demonstrate the supremacy of spiritual thought force over all apparent material resistance must necessarily depend upon your understanding of mental laws, their nature, and how they operate.

We must come to think of the mental medium, which is the Principle governing spiritual mind healing, in terms of exact law. Our text says at the top of page 78: *While we might think of It as the Mind of God, we could not think of It as the Spirit of God; for the Mental Medium is automatic, while the Spirit must be Self-Knowing.*

Let us then consider this all-important idea of God or Reality in the terms of an Infinite Knower and a Limitless Doer. Even at the expense of repeating one idea a great many times, we reaffirm the thought that the Universe as Pure Spirit is filled with warmth and color. It is illumined with the Divine Presence. It is filled with Divine Ideas. In other words we are surrounded by an atmosphere, a Presence in the universe which is conscious, alive, awake, and aware. In this Divine Presence we live and move and have our being, while It moves through us as inspiration, intuition, and illumination.

This Presence is God, the Living Spirit, Love, the Eternal Reality, the Supreme Being, with whom we communicate in prayer and meditation, and who in the silent places of the soul floods our minds with new and better ideals. (Turn to page 585 and read the definition of *Divine Ideal, Divine Influx,* and *Divine Mind:* and on the following page *Divine Principle,* that you may have still another presentation of the difference between God as Pure Spirit, and Mind as Absolute Law.)

PERSONAL WORD AND IMPERSONAL LAW

To think of the universe as Pure Spirit, to uplift the thought and open the consciousness to an influx of the Divine, is to achieve communion with God. This has been the office of prayer throughout the ages. It was this Divine Inspiration coming to him as a voice from the Invisible, emanating from the burning bush in the wilderness, to which Moses responded. The wilderness symbolizes the need which Moses felt for inspiration; it typifies the unproductive, uncultivated place of the mind, the extreme need of man met by the consuming fire of Love descending from Heaven.

Moses had gone out into the wilderness to meditate and pray. He sorely needed inspiration. Somehow in his meditation and prayer he must have so completely left the human will behind that the Divine could speak and make Itself heard. The burning bush signifies that any ordinary object of nature, even a wilderness shrub, is shot through with the warmth and color of Pure Spirit. In this way the most humble event may proclaim the omnipresence of Good. The weakest link of any chain of Cause and Effect may be so tempered by the flame of a new concept that it will have sufficient strength to bind the entire sequence together.

This is also the meaning of Jacob's experience with the angel at the Ford of the Jabbok. He wrestled with the angel of his better self until the day broke, bringing to him a consciousness of the nearness of the Divine. In such spiritual experiences of inner communion with the Most High, even our nearest and dearest cannot be present. But it is then that we receive the conviction that the power within us is the very Power of God.

Jacob's earlier experience on the road to Haran symbolized the same intimate truth. In the experience of aloneness with the Invisible, the soul bares itself to the Divine Influx, heaven and earth are joined together, angels ascend and descend the ladder of intuition. The messenger of Truth, the witness of God, the inspiration of the Almighty descends into our thought and we receive the assurance that the place where we are is the dwelling place of God.

We must be careful not to confuse the Divine Presence with the Universal Law. The Universal Law is a Way, a Principle, an immutable Cause and Effect. Our text points out that the Mental Medium is automatic, but you will notice in the second paragraph on page 78 these words: *As we examine the Subjective, we find*

PERSONAL WORD AND IMPERSONAL LAW

It to be both intelligent and conscious, without knowing that It is intelligent, and without being Self-conscious.

(Read carefully page 580 under the definitions of *Consciousness* and *Conscious Mind;* and under the General Summary, page 397, read paragraph 4 beginning: *The Universal Mind, in its subjective state, is what we mean by the Law of Mind;* and the paragraph beginning at the bottom of page 396 which tells us that while the Law of Mind is subjective, It has Infinite Intelligence.)

One of the most difficult things for us to understand is that while we may consciously deal with the Law, which is creative; may even definitely direct It and set Its creative intelligence in motion for our good, yet the Law is not self-conscious. In other words, even though this Law is intelligent and creative, even though It is conscious of our desire, It has no self-consciousness, no self-choice with regard to such desires. It must execute the directions given It by the self-knowing mind. It must respond to our word.

Jesus was so certain of this that he said, *Heaven and earth shall pass away, but my words shall not pass away.* What a marvelous conception of his unity with Good and his command of the Law! That is why Jesus was different from other men. *He taught them as one having authority, and not as the scribes.* This is why the wind and the waves obeyed his will. He received the inspiration from the Spirit, but he commanded the Law.

That is really what we do every day in all common occurrences in dealing with the laws of nature. We are so accustomed to the reaction of the laws with which we are familiar that we have never stopped to recognize that in using any law of nature we are dealing with a creative agency which knows what to do and how to do it, but which cannot possibly have any self-choice.

Electricity does not know whether it is boiling eggs or furnishing motive power for the streetcar, but we might truly say that in a certain sense it knows how to do these things; as a matter of fact it must do them. We do the deciding; it has power but no decision. It has authority but no volition. It is energy, but of itself remains undirected. It is subject to our desires, and as our text says (page 78): *If this were not true of the laws of nature, we could not depend upon them, we should be confronted with caprice.*

It is because we may depend upon the laws of nature that we can have a science. The Science of Mind is an exact science; it is subject to our conscious use; it is a principle of nature just as chemical affinity is a principle of nature. If we do not understand this we shall never be able to consciously demonstrate. We might, through the prayer of faith, arrive at a conclusion which would be beneficial, but to reproduce that conclusion at will, to reduce the occasional experience to a laboratory experiment which may be reproduced whenever and wherever we desire — that is a different thing. One is chance; the other is science. We must be scientific in our approach to the conscious use of the Law of Mind.

The Law of Mind is absolutely impersonal. Anyone who understands it may use it. Once set in motion it tends to produce a logical result. It proceeds in a mathematical manner to create, and unless the tendency set in motion is changed it will create the logical result of whatever idea is given to it. In our Textbook we read in the last paragraph on page 78: *We cannot destroy the Law but we can redirect Its movement.* In this concept lies the possibility of freedom from bondage, not that we can change the Law but that we can change Its direction.

The spirit of man, being some part of the Spirit of God, has Self-consciousness and Self-choice. The Law, having neither Self-consciousness nor Self-choice, automatically reacts to the Spirit. Therefore when you treat someone else you are really treating yourself, and we wish you to know from the very start that this is exactly the way the Law works. You will never have to go outside yourself to treat any person, place, or thing; to think it necessary would be to deny the Unity of Good and your access to the Universal Law of Cause and Effect. Within this one Law all events transpire. Emerson rightly said that history is the record of the doings of this Mind on our planet.

While the Law of Mind is a blind force, It is intelligent. We could make no greater mistake than to think that subconscious means unconscious. It does not. Subconscious means below the threshold of the conscious mind. As a matter of fact the Subjective Law of the Universe with which we deal in giving treatments has limitless intelligence and limitless power to proceed from cause to effect. It is the creative agency in the universe.

PERSONAL WORD AND IMPERSONAL LAW

You will notice in the third paragraph on page 79 that reference is made to this Principle as the thing we use in practice, and also that we are cautioned not to be superstitious in our reaction to the Law. Too much emphasis cannot be placed upon this, for if you wish to become a scientific practitioner you must be one who knows what you are doing, why you are doing it, and just how to do it. When you give a treatment to help someone who is sick or in need, no matter what the need may be, you must be conscious that you are making a definite statement in Mind and that Mind is the sole and only actor.

Principle acts upon your thought and projects it into the experience of the one toward whom you direct it. This is the whole theory of mental spiritual practice. This is the meaning of *Be still and know that I am God.* It was back of the illumined thought of Jesus when he said, *Ye shall know the truth, and the truth shall make you free.* The purpose of this course of lessons is to help you understand exactly how to use this Law for yourself and others. You must begin at once to be definite in your use of It, and today consciously set the Law in motion for yourself and for someone else.

At the top of page 80 we point out that God is threefold in His nature: God is Spirit or Self-Knowingness; God is Law or action; God is form or result. You will at once recognize this as the Trinity which has run through all great religions of the world. I do not know of any great system of spiritual thought which did not include some teaching of the Trinity. We call it *The Thing Itself, The Way It Works,* and *What It Does.*

The Thing Itself is Pure Spirit; *The Way It Works* is Absolute Law; and *What It Does* is to give form to substance which is within Itself. This form we call creation. Whenever the Spirit wills or knows, as a result of Its will the Law is set in motion and produces that which the Spirit knows.

God never could do anything which would contradict His own nature. Hence we are certain that God cannot will evil, lack, limitation, or fear, for such thoughts would be self-destructive. If you wish to discover what the will of God is, try to realize what the nature of God must be and then realize that the will of God can never contradict the nature of God.

PERSONAL WORD AND IMPERSONAL LAW

Turn to page 438 and read what is said under the heading *God Knows No Evil,* and also page 433 under the heading *Judge Not That Ye Be Not Judged.* These ideas, I think, will help you to see that the nature of God must be Truth, Beauty, and Peace; and if the will of God is always in tune with His nature, which reason, science, and revelation alike tell us must be, then we know that God cannot will evil.

If God cannot will evil, what is evil? On page 590 in the Glossary read the definition of *Evil.* You will learn that of itself it is not person, place, nor thing, and that it will disappear from our experience in exact proportion as we cease using destructive thoughts.

Evil is merely a misconception, a wrong way of using Good. God does not will limitation, because the nature of God is Infinite and that which is Infinite cannot will limitation. Nor is God limited merely because we accept what we call a small amount of good. There is just as much life in a flea as there is in an elephant. Size has no meaning to the Infinite. We outline our experience and call it size; we deny the good and call our experience evil; we put the wrong combinations of thoughts together and call the effect pain. But a reorganization of thought removes these discords, showing that the Eternal Reality is ever-present, ever-available. Emerson expressed this beautifully when he said, *The finite alone has wrought and suffered; the Infinite lies stretched in smiling repose.*

Next we turn to page 81, Chapter III, for the definition of Spirit; and to page 633 in the Glossary where *Spirit* is defined as *the Self-Knowing One.* This will help us to understand the conception of the Universe as one limitless sea of Life, animated by a Divine Presence which is the very essence of Life, of Truth, of Beauty, of Joy, of Peace, and of Perfection. While we cannot conceive of Spirit in Its entirety, in our highest moments of exalted thought we do feel this Divine and effulgent Presence. Let us realize that this Supreme Spirit is at the very center of our own being. *Closer is He than breathing, and nearer than hands and feet.*

If you will turn to page 364 under the heading *The Indivisible Whole* and read through to the top of page 368, you will find a complete description of what this living spiritual Presence has meant to those who have sensed Its divine immanence within themselves. Read also the definition of *Immanent* on page 600; and Jesus' idea of the *New Birth* as presented on page 471. Read also in the General Summary on page 421 the description of the teaching of this great mystic. All of this helps us to feel the reality of this Divine Spirit in which we are immersed and which finds an avenue of Self-expression through us.

The last paragraph on page 81 contains the statement: *The Spirit is Self-Propelling.* This means that all initiative proceeds from the Self-Knowing Mind. The Law never initiates anything; It always reacts to the Spirit. As you carefully read the first and second paragraphs on page 82, try to realize the meaning of this marvelous idea that Spirit is both the center and circumference of everything; that there is such a perfect completion within your own soul that you really do have access to the very Soul of the Universe. Daily practice calling upon this inner Intelligence in belief, in faith, in confidence, knowing that It will respond to you, that It will guide you.

We have already considered fully the section of our lesson at the bottom of page 82 and top of page 83, which is a further elaboration of the idea that the Spirit within you, the God within you, commands the Law, which is the Doer of the Word. Now you should immediately put this understanding which you have received into definite and conscious use. Of course you will realize that you may translate these thoughts into your own words, and that you should always use such words as have a definite meaning to your own consciousness, but the treatment should always be definite.

SUMMARY

There is an Infinite Knower and a Limitless Doer in the Universe. The Knower responds to us as feeling. The Doer is a mechanical reaction. These we call the Principle and the Presence. The Principle is the Law of Mind in Action; the Presence is the warmth and color of Infinite Intelligence, personal to each one of us, moving through us as inspiration, intuition, and illumination. Prayer is communion with the Divine Presence.

We never confuse the Presence with the Law or the Principle. The Law is always subjective or subconscious to our conscious thinking. That means it is like our own subconscious mind; it receives the impress of our thought, asking no questions and always tending to create a situation to correspond with our thinking. The subconscious or subjective law of the individual and the Universal are one and the same thing.

Even as there is such a subconscious law within us which we call our individual subconsciousness, we are surrounded by a Universal Law of like nature, and our individual subconsciousness is but a center of attraction and repulsion in It. This is certainly true of every other law in nature. Everyone uses the gravitational force, the same principle of electricity and mathematics, and all are guided by the same law and order. All that we do is individualize Universalities.

To understand a law of nature is to have a science relative to that law. It is the same with the Science of Mind. It is exact, and we must consciously use it and the Law for definite purposes. We should not leave this to chance but should always make it a question of choice. The Law, being impersonal, works the same for everyone, but the Spirit is personal to each one of us.

While the Law of Mind is a mechanical force, it is also intelligent and knows how to convert ideas into things. This Law with which we deal is not limited, and knows nothing about big or little, hard or easy, good or bad.

Remember we are talking about the Law. The Presence of the Living Spirit is an entirely different thing. It comes to all of us with warmth, color, and feeling, causing us to initiate new channels of causation in the Law which automatically responds to our thinking. Daily we should court the Presence of the Spirit and use the Law.

QUESTIONS

Brief answers to these questions should be written out by the student after studying this lesson, and the answers compared with those in the Appendix.

1. Upon what does our ability to demonstrate the Spiritual Law depend?

2. How should we think of the Principle of Spiritual Mind Healing?

3. How should we think of the Spirit of God?

4. How shall we commune with this Divine Spirit in an intimate way?

5. What does the burning bush which Moses saw represent?

6. What is the meaning of Jacob's experience with the Angel of God's Presence, and his experience on the road to Haran?

7. What do the ascending and descending angels represent?

8. How does the Universal Subjective Mind or Law respond to us?

9. Can Subjective Law refuse to act upon our thought?

10. What gave Jesus his authority?

11. (a) What gives us authority over any law of nature?
    (b) Is this true of mental law?

12. What is mental treatment?

13. Where does mental treatment take place?

14. Do the expressions *subconscious* and *unconscious* have the same meaning?

15. What constitutes scientific mental practice?

16. What do we mean by the Trinity?

17. (a) Can God will evil? If not, why not?
    (b) What, then, is evil and limitation?

18. What words and thoughts should be used in giving a mental treatment?

METAPHYSICAL INTERPRETATIONS OF THE BIBLE

based on

Thomas Troward's *Bible Mystery and Bible Meaning*

THE GREAT LAWGIVER

In beginning his discussion on the mission of Moses, Troward again points out that the Bible repeats its few grand principles over and over again, and that its teaching regarding man starts with two great facts, which are: *first,* that man is the likeness of God; *second,* that he individualizes the Creative Spirit in his own life. At first he is ignorant of this and consequently brings upon himself both trouble and limitation.

The whole theory of the Bible is based upon these simple propositions. Having shown in the story of The Fall what happens through a negative use of the power of thought, the rest of scripture is devoted to the winning of Redemption, which is the realization of the perfect Self, the archetypal man, or Christ incarnated within every soul.

Troward tells us that the mission of Moses was founded on the conception that God is One Self-Existent and Self-Transforming Power of which everything is some mode of manifestation: *. . . there is none beside me. . . .I am God, and there is none else* (Isaiah 45:21-22). This One, this God beside Whom there is none else, is the Universal Spirit. As Riley points out, *All the sacred books declare that God is One, the First and the Last, from Which nothing can be excluded and to Which nothing can be added.*

In an excerpt from the sacred books on the Fifty-seven Attributes of God, we read: *God is Breath of breath, Spirit, Primeval Fire, Creator and Generator, and being the One great Universal Supreme Soul, all things are threaded on God like pearls on a string. . . . The universe is spread in God's vast form and the Infinite One is the ocean into which all things flow.* From the text of Taoism: *The Tao, considered as unchanging, has no name.* Again from the same text: *That which made things and gave to each its character, was not Itself a thing.* In Hebrews 1:10 we read: *And, Thou, Lord, in the beginning hast laid the foundation of the earth; and the heavens are the works of thine hands.* And in Ephesians 4:6: *One God and Father of all, who is above all, and through all, and in you all.*

It is upon the union of our life with this eternal One that the teaching of Moses was based. The *I AM* Principle which he taught is both universal and individual. *I AM*, as Troward suggests, *is the announcement of Being in the Absolute . . . self-existence without limitation of either space or time.* It was the inspiration of Moses to perceive the meaning of the *I AM* in Its universal sense, the God who is over all and above all.

It was the spiritual genius of Jesus to perceive that the Universal *I AM* is reproduced in the individual *I*. He said, *I and my Father are one* (John 10:30). He knew that we must live in complete union with Good before the Power of the One can be delivered in Its fullness. Thus in *Fragments of a Faith Forgotten,* when they asked him when the kingdom of heaven should come he said, *When two shall be One and the without as the within, and the male with the female neither male nor female.* This refers to a consciousness of complete union between God and man.

In studying the lives of both Moses and Jesus we discover that while Moses taught the great Law of Cause and Effect, exemplified by the precept of an eye for an eye and a tooth for a tooth, Jesus, without denying the Mosaic Law, affirmed a Love guided by Wisdom.

Troward tells us that the teaching of the *I AM* had been familiar to Moses since his youth. This teaching was confined to those who had been initiated into the great mysteries of Osiris. Osiris is a symbol of the Higher Self in Egyptian mythology.

It was the mission of Moses, Troward tells us, to make known to the common people the mysteries of the Temple. It was his mission to teach not only that pure Spirit is the ultimate essence of all that is, but that man is included in this all. This Self is the Lord of all, the eternal Ruler, the Source of all things.

In the Upanishads the ancients taught that there is an Absolute Being subsisting under all appearances, but Itself never confined or conditioned to any experience. They also taught that as the individual attains truth and identifies himself with it, in that degree he passes into the Being of pure Spirit. The Gita says, *Perceiving the same Law present in everything and everywhere . . . and when he realizes perfectly that all things whatsoever in nature are comprehended in One, he attains to the supreme Spirit.*

Undoubtedly the Egyptian priests were well-versed in the knowledge of unity. They were also conscious of the psychic life, but just as Osiris represented the symbol of the higher Self or the Wisdom Principle, so the goddess Isis represented the Divine Mother or Bringer Forth. She is representative of what today we call the Subjective Principle. It is evident that even the idols of antiquity must have stood for some symbolic presentation of concealed wisdom.

While the chosen few had knowledge of psychic and spiritual facts, the vast majority were kept in ignorance. Moreover even the priesthood in the temples of Egypt, whose business it should have been to gradually acquaint the whole population with the truth, had themselves degenerated. They had practiced ceremonials without understanding their meaning, until finally the only power they exercised came closer and closer to what has been called *Egyptian Darkness.* Such knowledge as they possessed was exercised largely on the mental plane. And this is exactly what differentiated the teaching of Moses from that of the Egyptian priests who had forgotten the real meaning of *I AM.* Like those who preceded the symbolic Deluge, they had great knowledge of psychic powers but lacked the vision of spiritual realization. Unconscious of the Unity of Good they used such power as they had for evil purposes.

Symbolically, Moses represents the Higher Principle riding upon the seas of Egyptian darkness. Hence he is discovered in a little ark floating on the water. Since the Ark represents the Life Principle in Its transcendent or purely spiritual phase, and since in this instance water is symbolic of the Subjective Principle which is subject to confusion, the symbolic birth of Moses means the appearance of an individual who, while amply conscious of the subjective or psychic life (the realm of Cause and Effect operating as a Law of Mind), is equally conscious of the unifying and coordinating power of Spirit.

Whatever viewpoint one may take of ancient symbolism, nothing is more certain than that it taught a few central truths, one of which was the necessity that the Spirit shall dominate the mind. The child Moses is found floating upon the waters, just as the Ark floated on the sea, and we find the man Moses parting the waters of the sea. These are the waters that closed in upon the pursuing Egyptians, immersing and destroying them in its flood. Philo says, *In inward meaning, the flood is symbolically representative of spiritual dissolution.* Swedenborg says, *By the flood is signified an inundation of evil and falsity.* It was this psychic sea of illusion, also referred to as *Maya*, which Moses parted.

The occult knowledge of the Egyptian priests, their knowledge of psychic and mental powers, was tremendous. But being ignorant of or having forgotten the true significance of spiritual power which should be exercised only for beneficent purposes, they became swallowed up in the very power which they had generated, thus proving that the Law of Cause and Effect works with mathematical certainty. Jesus said, . . . *for all they that take the sword shall perish with the sword.*

It was the Staff of Moses, representing the authority of Divine Wisdom, the Word of God in Moses, the Divine Command of the Unity of God, which symbolically parted the sea of confusion, the sum total of all human error. And the Children of Israel, that is, the Children of the *I AM* (which signifies any and all who understand their true relationship to Spirit), walked through the Red Sea on dry land. The pursuing Egyptians, though filled with power, were also covered with confusion. Thus the Deluge — the story of the flood — repeats itself.

We have the same symbol in Zoroastrianism. Mazda is the father of justice. Mazda refers to the Light which overcomes darkness, or the Good which always triumphs over evil. In the same system of thought we have the Light or Truth, the Good completely subduing evil, confusion, and chaos, until finally the Light reigns supreme.

We find Jesus walking upon the water, putting under his feet the sum total of human ignorance, viciousness, and disunion. In Scott's *Lady of the Lake* the symbol is again repeated: *She is calm whatever storms assail the sea, and when the tempest rolls, hath power to walk the waters like our Lord.*

It was the mission of Moses, then, to lead the Children of Israel out of the darkness of the Egyptian night; to lead ignorance into enlightenment. But the Children of Israel murmured, hesitated, drew back. This represents the inertia of our own thought patterns, our habitual thought forms which bind us to superstition, fear, ignorance, and bondage.

When a modern metaphysician less than a hundred years ago spoke of the argument of error in the human consciousness, many intellectuals may have smiled. And yet today psychology recognizes what it calls the inertia of thought patterns; that which appears to be an argument emanating from these subjective habitual states of thought. To dislodge these thought patterns is one of the most difficult tasks of the psychologist.

It was the mission of Moses to lead the Children of the *I AM,* those who understood their relationship to God, not only out of the material bondage of objective slavery, but equally out of the psychic bondage of subjective slavery. Maya, or the great illusion, was to be penetrated. And what was this illusion other than the belief in their separation from Good. The Great Exodus represents a symbolic rising from the lower to the higher nature, led by an intuitional sense of unity. It was following the Feast of the Passover that this exodus began. The Feast of the Passover is a symbol representing a realization of Truth. It is a symbolic repast of the fruits of Spirit.

The march through the wilderness represents a march through the desolate places of the soul — fear, superstition, want, famine, hunger, and anything that stands for the illusion of separation — to the Promised Land filled with fruit and honey. It is a march from the valley to the mountain top, which means from the lower to the higher nature.

You will remember that Moses was told that everything his eye looked upon his feet would tread upon. This means that what he beheld with undimmed spiritual vision, he would come into possession of. This, of course, is a statement of cause and effect, as were most of the teachings of Moses.

Troward draws an interesting comparison between the teachings of Moses and those of Jesus. It was, he said, the mission of Moses to lead the Children of the *I AM* (that is, those who recognize their unity with Good) out of the wilderness of their own fear, ignorance, and confusion into the Promised Land of Truth, Beauty, and Light. And it was the mission of Jesus to continue in the footsteps of Moses and in some way repeat the Exodus and reestablish the people of the *I AM*. Hence we find Jesus laying great stress on the Law and the Prophets, on the Law of Cause and Effect, on everything that Moses taught, but tempering the Law of Justice with the realization that Love ever seeks to guide us into pathways of Peace, Joy, and Perfection.

Troward tells us that the English version of the Bible which states that Jesus said, *If ye believe not that I am he, ye shall die in your sins,* is misquoted. What Jesus actually said was, *Except ye believe that* I AM, *ye shall die in your sins.* Now this passage means that unless you believe in the Eternal Principle within you as one of complete unity, Divine guidance, etc., you will continue making mistakes. For sin means making a mistake or missing the mark. From the Mahabharata: *In consequence of ignorance, one sinks into hell. Ignorance is the swing of misery. Through ignorance one suffers afflictions and encounters great dangers.* Dying in your sins has no reference to a theological damnation.

Purgatory is symbolic of the purification that is brought about as the fire of Spiritual Truth burns out the dross of human experience. Clement of Alexandria tells us: *The fire of purgatory is the rational spiritual fire that penetrates the soul.* Origen said, *Each sinner himself [which means each person in his own mistakes] lights the flame of his own fire . . . his conscience is agitated and pierced by its own pricks.* Plotinus tells us that purgatory is a way of purification from earthly desires. Hence when Jesus said in effect that except you believe that *I AM* you shall continue to suffer, he was teaching the Law of Cause and Effect. In this he was continuing the teaching of Moses, for it was his mission not only to continue the teaching of the *I AM* but to explain it in terms of its meaning to the individual life. Troward tells us that if *I AM* is the generalized statement of God, it must also be the generalized statement of Man, for man is the image and likeness of God.

The whole teaching of Jesus in following out the instructions of Moses was to show that what is true about God is also true about Man. God is at the center of every man's life. Jesus came, as Troward said, *not to proclaim Himself, but Man; not to tell us of His own Divinity separating Himself from the race and making Him the Great Exception, but to tell us of our Divinity and to show in Himself the Great Example of the* I AM *reaching its full personal expression in Man.*

THE GREAT LAWGIVER

We find, then, that as it was the mission of Moses to proclaim the Universal Principle of the eternal *I AM,* so it was the purpose of the teaching of Jesus to show the intimate relationship between the Universal and the personal; to show us that our very life is in essence some part of the Being of God, and that whatever we believe does for us in very fact exist.

The Egyptians believed in the power of darkness, so out of the creative fertility of their own imagination such an apparent power was conjured up that it confused both themselves and their enemies. Moses perceived that there could be no power of darkness operating against the Light; that the people of the *I AM* who believed in the Unity of Good were guided by this Unity in which they believed.

The wrong use of the Law of Cause and Effect is called sin or the transgression of the Law. This produces suffering and death, or dissolution, while the knowledge of Truth always produces a resurrection. As Troward points out, *the transgression . . . is the transgression of the Law of the* I AM *in ourselves.* Our punishment does not come from God, who is Good, nor does the Law, which is merely a Law of Cause and Effect, hold anything against us. Our punishment is an inevitable result of the use we have made of the Law of Cause and Effect.

Hear, O Israel: the Lord our God is one Lord (Deuteronomy 6:4). If God is the Only Being, *I AM* must be the name of this Being, and the conscious knowledge of the meaning of *I AM* is the keynote of liberty. The transgression, Troward tells us, is in supposing there is any power opposed to Good. Once we see through this proposition and realize that there is nothing opposed to Good, but that the Eternal *I AM* is Wisdom, Truth, Love, and Beauty forever guiding us, then we are made free. But in such degree as we limit the *I AM* we are limiting ourselves.

When we think of the *I AM* as separate from our own being we feel that we are isolated, each on his own so to speak, disconnected from the central Power. It is necessary for us to understand with Moses that the *I AM* is Universal, and to understand with Jesus that the Universal is individualized through, in, and as our own nature. Obeying this nature we are automatically saved or resurrected from our previous mistakes.

In simple, actual, and direct mental practice this would mean that we should daily affirm our union with God, our oneness with the Creative Genius of the Universe, and that we consciously believe and understand that we are Divinely guided, guarded, protected; that everything we do is made whole, prosperous, and happy.

DESIRE, OPINION, AND REVELATION

It was John who said, and rightly, *Believe not every spirit, but try the spirits whether they are of God.* Paul said, *God is not the author of confusion, but of peace.* Possibly he knew that our conscious opinions and our subjective desires so frequently confuse the revelations that when an alleged revelation appears it is so distorted with conflicting opinions that much of its truth is lost.

If we were to put all of the alleged revelations of the ages together we would be amazed to find how contradictory they are. In fact the contradictions would be so complete that practically the whole revelation would be wiped out, and this in face of the fact that each prophet claims to have received his inspiration directly from the Mind of God. The confusion of such alleged revelations is so great that intelligence compels us to put up the sign: *Stop, Look, and Listen.*

We are amazed to discover that some of these revelations which seem to come from God stimulate man to commit the most atrocious crimes, for many crimes that have been committed in the name of Liberty have also been committed in the name of Truth.

It stands to reason that the Author of Peace cannot inspire confusion. And God is the Author of Peace, since a house divided against itself cannot stand. If God stands for that which is rational, the essence of Peace and Poise; if the Divine means Love, Beauty, Harmony, and Reason, it follows that from this Divine Fountain only pure waters can flow. God could not be the author of confusion inspiring men to acts of destruction. God could not be the author of confusion leading men to irrational mental or spiritual conclusions. Therefore a person who would differentiate between subjective hallucination and opinion, between desire and reality, does well to analyze his own feelings, emotions, and mental reactions. And he does well to analyze the reactions of other people, regardless of whether they are numbered among the so-called great, the little known, or even the unknown.

In the pursuit of Truth one seeks to wed oneself to reason, for she is the only mistress who can lead the soul to the altar of Reality. We do not dispute the idea of revelation, since all truth is some revelation of Reality to the mind of man. We do not deny that there is a Spirit which inspires and a Guidance which directs. What we say is that when it seems as though this Guidance directs us chaotically or counsels men to destructive acts, it is not Divine Guidance at all. It is some form of opinion or desire masquerading as reason, seeking to justify itself by claiming to be the Voice of God.

When someone tells you that he has received a revelation direct from the Almighty you will be wise if you analyze his revelation and see whether it really is inspired by the Divine or whether it is merely a rationalization of his own desire. History records many so-called revelations by which men have claimed to be directed by God to commit such atrocious crimes that sensitiveness shrinks from the fact and intelligence refuses to accept the verdict.

Life cannot will death. Death is the direct opposite of life. Therefore Jesus said, *God is not the God of the dead, but of the living.* Jesus with his clear comprehension of Reality knew that Life cannot will death, but many lesser prophets have proclaimed that the Divine Being inspired them to kill. Most nations at war, worshiping tribal gods, react from their collective unconscious with this same motivation. But whether it be an individual or a collective unconscious, the principle operating is the same.

We may be certain that when Cyrus mounted his chariot and rode in front of his legions crying, "Kill! Kill! Kill! and to God be the glory!" after having attended the divinations of the oracle, what he was really proclaiming, but of course unconsciously, was: "Kill! Kill! Kill! and to Cyrus be the glory!" Even this barbarian shrank in horror before the terrific carnage about to take place. His desire had first to be rationalized in order that his opinion might be justified; therefore he had to receive, through his imagination, evidence for the belief that his killing of men was done for the glory of God and not for the glory of Cyrus.

We take this instance, so far removed from us personally and from our present history, that we may be impersonal about it. But every day this same performance takes place in our own consciousness. We certainly should realize that all is not revelation which masquerades under its name. In the present day when we are privileged to understand more about psychic reactions, history is better explained on the basis of human will to power.

Today more than ever psychic revelations are imposed upon our consciousness through the sincerity of those receiving such messages in automatic writings, in seances, and by various other media through which such revelations come, and again we must put up the sign: *Stop, Look, and Listen.* To one who has, over a period of many years, carefully studied such apparent revelations, it is evident that too frequently these revelations are largely governed by the mental background of the one through whom they come. Generally we find in them elements of philosophies, the religions, the social, political, and economic systems which the author has believed in or theorized over, toward which he has aspired, or in which he was born. This in no way contradicts the sincerity of those through whom these messages come. Therefore it is not a question of condemning or criticizing the individual; it is merely a question of right judgment and a sane perspective.

We certainly should believe in no revelation which contradicts the final Unity, Goodness, and Perfection of the Supreme Being. In analyzing such revelations we should carry them right back to the point of reason and unity, and whenever they contradict reason we may know that they are not revelations but hallucinations or the rationalizations of desire. They may emanate directly from the consciousness of an individual or from the conscious reactions of an entire race.

We are told that Martin Luther saw the devil. One day he presented himself in Luther's study. Now what was it that this reverend gentleman saw? Not an actual devil, since intelligence compels us to admit that the devil is a mythological figure with no reality outside man's consciousness.

What Luther saw was a personification of the then universal belief about the devil. If we could ask the average man of that period what the devil looked like, his description would be similar to what Luther saw. Strange as it may seem, what he saw was an idea, but this idea had its roots deeper than his own personal consciousness. It arose from the sum total of the opinion of his day. Everybody believed the devil looked like that; therefore the devil did look like that in belief, and what Luther saw was the belief personified; a picture in imagination, but a picture of an imagination more real than his personal ne, more dynamic than his individual thought. This picture was impressed upon his psyche, and in some moment when he was subjective to it, it appeared.

With all sincerity Luther may have believed that he saw an actual devil, but with equal sincerity the man who is suffering from an hallucination believes that he sees some grotesque form. It is real enough as far as the experience is concerned, but it is nevertheless an illusion as far as reality is concerned. Luther and all his contemporaries believed in an actual devil, and what they believed in he saw. Hence, seeing, he doubly believed.

This is one of the reasons why many people believe that God ordains suffering, impoverishment, and unhappiness, and that He even demands murder. When we subject such a concept to the rule of reason and common sense we soon discover that the All-Creative Principle could not will martyrdom, suffering, or impoverishment, for this would not be to the glory, but to the degradation of the Creative Principle. God would not be honored, but dishonored; not made whole, but limited.

Yet what countless thousands of sincere and well-meaning persons suffer the illusion of such a belief and actually condemn the desire for happiness in this world. The very thought of the crucifixion of Jesus has, in innumerable instances, stimulated such morbid introspection that the resurrected form of Christ is but dimly seen through the clouds of darkness and despair. Too often the cross and the tomb overshadow the resurrection.

We must not forget that when we are dealing with this psychic life of ours we are dealing with a very tricky thing. It will just as quickly provide us with an illusion as with a reality. But deeper than this psychic life there is a Spiritual Intelligence which transcends even our objective processes of reasoning, and it can distinguish between illusion and reality.

Our subconscious reactions will coerce us unless we control them, will cause us to believe all kinds of fantastic things unless reason sits in judgment. Therefore we should be careful at all times to study any alleged revelation in the light of this truth, knowing as we do that one's personal opinion may masquerade as any revelation which one's unconscious desire may order, for the entire race thought is more or less active in all of us.

DESIRE, OPINION, AND REVELATION

One of the most prolific fields for race hallucination, strange as it may seem, is in the field of so-called revealed religion. Accumulated acceptances of pronounced beliefs have finally created such a subjective reaction to them that people believe all sorts of things, reasonable and unreasonable. Usually it takes a strong new belief to shatter the old. Fortunately, back of most revelations, especially the great spiritual ones, there has always been enough reality, that is, enough of the nature of Truth has been revealed, not only to give vitality to the belief but to equip it with power and give it a performance which has been good.

Thus in analyzing the great revelations we do not need to recheck them in their entirety, but merely to recheck those parts which arise from human opinion, human desire, or psychological rationalization.

We shall find that reality is at least partly revealed through most of these great systems of thought, but we shall also find a great deal of illusion. Nowhere was this more apparent than in the ancient caste system, which did not rise out of reality since there can be no God who holds one person superior to another. It was an economic thing, and what is more natural than that the dominant minded should have rationalized their desire and even had it seemingly revealed to them that some were of lower origin than others, and therefore were outcasts. In Psalm 82:6 we read: *I have said, Ye are gods; and all of you children of the most High.* In the days of slavery in America many of our Southern brethren rationalized their belief in slavery as God's will. It could not be the will of God that some men should be free while others were bound, since God is the Author of freedom and not of bondage.

It is interesting to note with what dynamic authority many of our so-called great seers have spoken. With sincere conviction they have proclaimed, "Thus saith the Lord." It was not until the advent of science that reason began to deny these theological assumptions. Science deals with facts and not with opinions, and must reduce these facts into principles which never vary and which are always impersonal.

With the advent of science we have the beginning of the destruction of superstition. This does not mean that science will destroy religion. Nothing can do that, for true religion is man's immediate experience of Reality. Science will merely destroy distorted beliefs, and in so doing it will render true religion a great service since it will reveal the nature of Reality to be entirely impersonal, responsive alike to each and to all.

As science proclaims the rule of reason and a government of law, new revelations come. These new revelations, even as the old, the student of Truth must carefully scrutinize. He must remain master in his own household. Unless he does so he will be a mental puppet dancing to other people's thoughts, coerced by the ideas which have already hypnotized them, and if the blind lead the blind, shall they not both fall into the ditch?

BIBLES OF THE WORLD

Fragments from the spiritual history of the race revealing the fundamental Unity of religious thought and experience.

TAOISM

The right way leads forward; the wrong way backward. Do not proceed on an evil path. Do not sin in secret. Accumulate virtue. Increase merit. Turn toward all creatures with a compassionate heart.

Assist those in need; and rescue those in danger.

Regard your neighbor's gain as your own gain; and regard your neighbor's loss as your own loss.

CONFUCIANISM

Put away evil without hesitation. Do not carry out plans, the wisdom of which you have doubts.

The way of the superior man is threefold: virtuous, he is free from anxieties; wise, he is free from perplexities; bold, he is free from fear.

BUDDHISM

The giving hand, the kindly speech, the life of service, impartiality to one as to another: — these be the things that make the world go round.

Growth in faith, growth in virtue, growth in insight: — these are the three attainments.

JUDAISM and CHRISTIANITY

Execute true justice, and show mercy and compassion every man to his brother.

And oppress not the widow, nor the fatherless, the stranger, nor the poor; and let none of you imagine evil against his brother in your heart.

Be perfect, be of good comfort, be of one mind, live in peace; and the God of love and peace shall be with you.

HINDUISM

The peaceful mind soon becomes well-established in wisdom.

Like the body that is made up of different limbs and organs, all mortal creatures exist depending upon one another.

LESSON 5

SPIRIT

Its Meaning, Action, and Use

A Message from Ernest Holmes

One of the principal things you will learn in this lesson is that you are not concentrating any power when you use the Science of Mind, but rather through belief and faith and communion with the Spirit in you and around you, you are using a Power that is already centered everywhere. You do not have to take It from one place to another. What you are learning is that you use this Power at the very center of your own being, for this is the only place that you meet the Divine Presence or use the Universal Principle, and it is always a combination of these two fundamental realities with which you are dealing.

We have discovered that some people wait for years before they realize the simplicity of this thing. We trust that you are not such a person and that you have already proved to some degree that you do not wish, will, supplicate, coerce, or concentrate anything; that you do not send out thoughts, or hold thoughts, or influence people. Your prayers, your thoughts, your beliefs, your affirmations, your treatments are all at the center of your own being. They could be nowhere else.

But what does this mean other than the act of convincing yourself? The only reason that this sometimes seems difficult is that there are so many unconscious denials in every man's life. As you penetrate these and rise to an attitude of simple acceptance you will get remarkable results.

We wish you all the success in the world in doing this.

SPIRIT

Its Meaning, Action, and Use

(textbook reference: pages 83-87)

As already explained in our previous lessons, creation does not mean making something out of nothing. Creation means the giving of form to the formless. It is the act whereby the invisible becomes visible. Turn to the Glossary and read the definition of *Creation* and *the Creative Medium*. You will notice that the first definition contains the thought that creation is God making something out of Himself by becoming the thing He creates. It is necessary for us to conceive of a single Power which, by the act of mental projection within Itself, gives birth to form.

The paragraph headed *The Endless Creation* (page 492) makes clear the fact that while particular objects may have a beginning and an end, yet creation itself is endless. This gives a new meaning to the old phrase, *World without end*. This endless creation is a continuous mental projection of the Universe within Itself.

This mental projection within the One is what is meant by the Word of God, the Contemplation of Spirit, the Self-Recognition of Reality. This we must keep in mind when we seek to demonstrate or prove our Principle in actual practice. We must be sure that the thought will give rise to the form. In order to do this, in our imagination we must resolve things into thoughts and thoughts into things. This is what might be called making a mental diagnosis of wrong conditions in order that we may treat them scientifically and effectively to make them right. We must realize that the Spirit is the Active Principle, and that, as our lesson explains, all else is subject to Its will.

In order that you may understand this more fully turn to the section dealing with *The Law of Correspondents* (page 483). You will note that back of every visible form there is a mental concept or thought form which is an exact counterpart of the object. The subjective word is the Word of Causation and it contains a picture of the objective. In fact the objective world is really a manifestation of the subjective world. The thought and the thing are but the two ends of the same sequence.

This subjective world is the medium of Law. Into it we drop the images of thought which tend to objectify in our experience. It is desirable that we know how to use this Power and how to control It in order that we may actually get the most out of life. (See page 29, *Limitless Power at Man's Disposal.*) We are really using this Divine Creative Power every time we think. The only way to stop using It is to stop thinking, and that is impossible. What we all wish to do is to use this limitless Power consciously and constructively for definite purposes.

We spoke in a previous paragraph of a changing universe. This idea of change is dealt with under the heading *Spirit, the Changeless* (page 83). The Creative Principle is conscious of that which It manifests; but It is not conscious of any effort or process in Its manifestation. For instance, when we plant a seed in the ground we are invoking the creative agency of the soil, which in conjunction with sun, rain, and atmosphere will produce a plant for us. The process whereby the seed unfolds into a plant is a mechanical and not a self-conscious one. It is its nature to do this according to a certain mathematical law, the law of evolution.

Involution is conscious. Evolution is automatic. We must never forget this when we come to the point of treating either ourselves or others. We plant the seed; the Law of Mind produces the desired result. We do not have to be conscious of the process, but we should be conscious of the idea we desire to see projected into our experience.

The Law of the Lord being perfect, it is our business to believe that It is working for us and not against us. On page 414, the first paragraph, are these words: *Effective treatment must be independent of any existing circumstances.* This means that when you give a treatment you must know what you wish to have done or what you desire the effect to be, but the treatment itself must be given in complete independence of anything that now exists in your experience. This of course calls for faith, but in this instance you will find it is a faith based on understanding rather than superstition. It is faith reduced to science.

Let us examine another thought in this same paragraph: *From this viewpoint there is no hard and no easy.* How wonderful it will be when we no longer think that one thing in our spiritual work is hard and another is easy. Since with God all things are possible, since the Law of the Lord is perfect, and since there is a Perfect Presence and a Perfect Principle, what more could we desire? We are not to think of some things being hard while others are easy, but we are to know that the Truth responds immediately and perfectly to any demand made upon It.

Because this is true, and because the Law works impersonally and automatically, we can see that negative impulses will produce results as surely as positive ones. Therefore we need to watch the character and quality of our thought. Attention is drawn to this idea in the second paragraph of page 412 in these words: *The objective form to which we give our attention is created from the very attention which we give to it.* In other words, to look at a wrong condition and to fear it is to perpetuate it. To contemplate limitation is to create it.

Jesus told us that when we pray we must enter the closet and shut the door. We should approach life inwardly and not outwardly, for to look only at the outward is to perpetuate the form we desire to dissolve. Here is the crux of the whole matter. On what is our faith and confidence based? Surely not on outward appearance, but on inward Reality. This is why we are told never to count our enemies, but as Isaiah said, *Look unto me* [the God within], *and be ye saved.* How well this spiritual genius knew what he was talking about and how wise for us to follow his example! His contemplation of the Perfection of God, and the fact of man's unity with God led to demonstrations of healing and deeds of power.

Read the section on page 456 headed *As Little Children.* We should cultivate the acceptance of the little child. We must learn to believe, for as Jesus said, *Go thy way; and as thou hast believed, so be it done unto thee* (Matthew 8:13). Today you should not only believe but begin to practice what you have already learned. No matter what else you do, be sure to take ten or fifteen minutes twice a day to center your thought serenely and peacefully on the invisible, and to believe that the form of experience which you wish in your life is being created for you. Mentally see its objective manifestation. Accept it completely and try never to deny it, for this is correct practice.

It may assist you to obtain inner conviction if you contemplate the words: *God, the Self-Existent First Cause, speaks and it is done.* (page 84). Intelligence decrees and the Immutable Law executes. We must use this Law definitely and consciously. For as individualizations of the Self-Existent Spirit, we decree, and the Law executes our commands. But read page 51 and you will realize that we know only as much as we can prove by actual demonstration.

Throughout the period of study based on these lessons and in your daily experience from now on, believe that you can demonstrate. (Read the definition of *Demonstration* on page 583.) We need to prove the Principle. It is easy to believe in an underlying Power or Principle in the Universe which governs all things and is all-powerful, but for ourselves *it is not enough to confess that God is the only Power there is* (page 563). In our personal experience, at least, we must prove the supremacy of Good over apparent evil. We must prove that the God-Principle is in us and so is available to us. We must recognize our Unity with the Divine Principle of Being.

If we look at Love long enough we shall become lovely (page 491). It is not enough merely to declare that God is Love. This was true before we made the declaration. Whatever statements we may make about the Divine Being in a treatment, we must unify with It inwardly in thought and imagination, or the treatment will not be complete and effective. If you say that there is only One Life and that Life is the Life of God, you have made an abstract statement about a Universal Principle. When you add "That Life is my life now," you have connected this Principle with your own experience; you have unified with It. Be sure to do this every day.

God speaks, and it is done. God, the Universal Mind, is manifest in man, the individual mind. Man is an individualized center of God-Consciousness; he repeats the Divine Creative Order in his own experience, but he must learn to identify his experience with his desire. That is why we say, *In practice we state clearly in words what these ideas mean to us and then we relate these statements to some needed experience or to some desired good which we have not been experiencing* (page 410). Unless we learn to do this definitely our statements will be up in the air instead of being clear and concrete. Just an abstract statement such as "God is all the Power there is," even though it is true, will not demonstrate the good we desire.

SPIRIT

The abstract statement of a fundamental truth and the realization of its meaning generate Spiritual Power, but do not distribute It. As with electricity we must not only generate power but we must direct it. Our conscious statements and acceptances give conscious direction to the Power generated. *There is One Life, that Life is God.* This is true. But we must complete the statement by distributing It, by saying, *That Life is my life now.*

An additional statement in regard to the matter of demonstration is found on page 84: *We have, then, an Infinite Spirit and an Infinite Law . . . Intelligence and the Way It works. God working through Law, which is unfailing and certain.* We must realize that it is this God-Principle within us which is the Power back of our thought. We must never try to hold thoughts or will things to happen. Do not even try practicing any form of mental concentration, for without any desire to criticize these methods we wish you to understand that they are not what we are trying to teach.

We are trying to teach you how to become a practitioner, how to demonstrate in your everyday experience the fact that you can produce results by calling upon a higher Creative Power, without any act of coercion or concentration. The Power is already concentrated and needs but to be definitely used. What does a gardener concentrate when he plants his crop? He does not concentrate anything. He plants the seed, that is all. You must use the Power that is within you. Be sure to make conscious use of this Power; otherwise you will reap no advantage for yourself from this study, nor will you be able to help anyone else. Of course you will endeavor to use it both for yourself and those who come to you for help. The Power is within you, and *Today is the day of salvation.*

The whole action of Spirit must be within Itself (page 84). I suppose that one of the most difficult things to thoroughly understand is the simplicity of the operation of the Law which we are using. It is just the interaction between thought and the Law. We might state the Principle in this way: God moves upon God, Spirit moves upon Itself, Life sets Its own Law in motion and out of Itself produces form. This is the art, the act, and the science of all creation.

Spirit moved upon the face of the deep. How marvelous and exalting is this idea of Reality, for we also move upon the face of the deep and out of the seeming void form emerges. Both cause and effect are spiritual. Read the last two paragraphs on page 413 and carefully consider the meaning of the words you will find there, because they are fraught with the utmost significance in your everyday practice.

An excellent method of procedure for your mental work will be found on page 49 under the heading *Hope a Subtle Illusion*. The Spirit creates by Self-Contemplation, that is by Self-Knowingness, and because we are Spirit our Self-knowingness also creates. *And the Word was with God, and the Word was God.* This word is your good, or rather the use you make of the God-Self within you. *I and my Father are one.* A knowledge of this was the secret of the power of Jesus.

Jesus exercised an authority in the invisible world which the Centurion recognized and at which he marveled. Read the account of this most interesting incident on page 437 and you will see that Jesus exercised actual authority on the invisible plane, but he did it with the utmost simplicity. He knew the secret of power (page 431). The Secret Place of the Most High was to him a place where he daily walked and communed with the Invisible Presence. Thus do the meek inherit the earth (page 427).

In the second and third paragraphs on page 85, carefully consider the idea of the original Energy and Intelligence moving as a mathematical law. As you consider the meaning of the last two lines in the third paragraph, *the Infinite or abstract Essence of concrete personality, and the Cause of all objective and subjective manifestation,* realize that this means that the Invisible Principle acts through the Immutable Law. This is also invisible but creates form because the Word always tends to produce form. This is the meaning of the statement in John: *And the Word was made flesh, and dwelt among us.*

In paragraph 2, page 395 you will find the thought that the Universal Mind can do for us only that which we know It is doing. The very fact that we are made out of Spirit presupposes the thought that we are free to express liberty or bondage. As a matter of fact both liberty and bondage come from the same source, being different degrees of the same thing. Since Reality Itself knows no big and no little, and since we give form to It in our own experience, we give to the form of our experience the size which we conceive mentally from day to day.

For instance, you will find that on some days you will do better work than on others. Thought is always creative, but some days your thought will conceive of a greater good than at other times. The more positive and certain it is the more effective it will be, but the movement of your thought will always be mathematical. That movement takes place in a mechanical field of Cause and Effect — intelligent, responsive, but unvolitional.

You must decide what you wish to have happen. Be sure it is in accord with the nature of Harmony and then convince yourself that this desired good is already an experience in your life. This is the secret of spiritual mind healing and demonstration. To believe more in the Invisible than in the visible and to judge not according to appearances, but to judge aright, is to use the Principle which gave Jesus his power. You doubtless understand this, but how effective is understanding unless you use it? Our motto should always be: *To do is to know.*

No limit can be placed upon the spirit of man (page 87). We should place no limit on the possibility of our use of this Divine Power. *If God be for us, who can be against us?* Therefore let us turn to the source of all personal power, the Infinite Spirit which has Its Being at the center of our own life, and daily in meditation commune with It.

SUMMARY

Creation is the manifestation of Spirit in form and is eternally going on. We are always creating something. Creation itself is an automatic, mechanical, and mathematical response to our thinking. We may choose what we want to think, but the Law cannot refuse to accept what we think. Thoughts and things are but two ends of the same proposition. Since it is impossible to stop thinking, we cannot stop creating. Our choice is whether we shall create constructively or destructively.

There should be no more effort in this process than there is in planting a seed. The Law of Creativity responds to us in the way we approach It. We can reduce faith and prayer to an exact science when we know how the Law of Mind works.

The more attention we give to negative conditions the more they will become associated with our thinking. It may be difficult to turn from appearance, but it is necessary. Each deals with the Divine Presence and the Creative Law in the silence of his own mind as he shuts the door to outward appearances and accepts his Unity with the Whole.

You will never know that this is true until you try it. It must pass from theory into practice. You must prove this Principle in your personal experience and in helping others, for this is the purpose of your study.

It is not enough merely to state an abstract principle or to say that God is all there is, for while this is true it is not making a definite use of the Law of Mind in Action. But because the Principle exists, or because God is all there is, you can both know God and use the Principle.

QUESTIONS

Brief answers to these questions should be written out by the student after studying this lesson, and the answers compared with those in the Appendix.

1. What is meant by creation?

2. What is meant by the endless creation?

3. What do we mean by resolving things into thoughts?

4. How does the practice of resolving things into thoughts apply to mental science?

5. What is meant by mental diagnosis?

6. What do we mean by mental correspondents?

7. When do we use the Divine Creative Power?

8. What do we mean by involution?

9. What do we mean by evolution?

10. What do we mean by faith reduced to science?

11. What do we mean by *entering the closet and closing the door* when we pray?

12. What is meant by *Intelligence decrees and Law executes*?

13. What is meant by a unity of thought and imagination in treatment?

14. What does *man as a creative center of God-Consciousness* mean?

QUESTIONS

15. Why is it that abstract statements, without specific realization and direction, will not demonstrate?

16. Why must we make conscious use of the Creative Power of Mind?

17. Why are both Cause and Effect spiritual?

18. What was the secret of the power of Jesus?

19. What is meant by *energy and intelligence moving as mathematical law?*

20. Why do we get better results through mental treatment on some days than on others?

METAPHYSICAL INTERPRETATIONS OF THE BIBLE

based on

Thomas Troward's *Bible Mystery and Bible Meaning*

THE GREAT WAYSHOWER

The point that Troward stresses in Chapter V, *The Mission of Jesus*, is: *Universal Mind, as the all-pervading, undistributed Creative Power, must be subjective mind . . . its relation to the individual mind must always be in exact correspondence to what the individual mind conceives of it.*

It was the mission of Moses to teach the Universal Law of Cause and Effect. It was the mission of Jesus not only to continue this teaching of the Law of Cause and Effect, but to show how it can be more intimately applied to individual and human relationships. He added beauty to power, and put feeling into that which of itself is merely a mechanical law. The Law of Mind, being a Doer and not a Knower, automatically responds to us by corresponding with our mental attitudes.

One of the chief difficulties in presenting the Science of Mind is the tendency which people have to confuse the laws of nature with the Spirit. When we speak of the Law of Mind as being a blind force, people are liable to think we are speaking of God, the Spirit, as merely a blind force. We should be careful to differentiate between the Law as a Way, and the Spirit as a Presence. It is from this Divine Presence that we receive inspiration, illumination, intuition, and guidance. As this inspiration images itself in our thought, its reflection is automatically cast into the Law which responds by corresponding.

Troward points out that we may view the Universal *I AM* as merely an unconscious Force which blindly follows our dictation without any sense of responsibility, or we may view It as being the only Principle which has decision and will, thus reducing the individual to a mechanical automaton. Or again we may view the Spirit as forever flowing into our spirit, merging with it. This enables us to set in motion sequences of causation, which we have decided we wish to experience. When our thought has been built on a conscious recognition of the Unity of Good, this sequence of Cause and Effect will never be destructive.

THE GREAT WAYSHOWER

Troward tells us that the Bible teaches that *from the center of his own smaller circle of perception the individual is free to make any selection that he will, and if he acts from a clear recognition of the true relations of things, the first use he will make of this Power will be to guard himself against any misuse of It. . . .* We must all come to see with Emerson that there is One Mind common to all individual men. Moreover, as Troward points out, we must come to realize *a higher and more far-seeing Wisdom* than that which we consciously possess. We must believe in Divine Guidance, and have complete trust in the Universal Creative Spirit as an active Presence of Consciousness and Intelligence, and the Universal Law as a servant of both God and man. We must come to see that God and man are One.

Troward makes plain that the institution of sacrifice is the most effective way of impressing the proper mental attitude on people's thoughts, because it implies the desire of the worshiper to submit himself to Divine Guidance. It is not that the All-Supreme Wisdom demands this recognition, but because such recognition is necessary if we are to consciously unify ourselves with the All-Power as well as the All-Wisdom.

Sacrifice symbolizes the offering of the lower self to the Higher. It symbolizes the surrender of the human to the Divine. It means the transmutation of lower qualities, animal desires, into a new birth. It signifies a condition of spiritual improvement as a result of having made the sacrifice. The burnt offering signified purification by fire, by which lower qualites were transmuted into higher ones. As the intellect advances in its evolution, it begins to realize that the sacrifice of animals, *the blood of bulls and goats, and the ashes of a heifer can have no power in themselves.* We awake to the realization that this cruder form of sacrifice is no longer necessary, and we say with the Psalmist, *Burnt offering and sin offering hast thou not required.* But instead of these, *I delight to do thy will, O my God; yea, thy law is within my heart.*

Troward states that the act of sacrifice carries with it the idea of making a covenant with God. Covenant means recognizing the true relationship between the Divine and the human as something which is eternally taking place. And I will establish my covenant with thee. This is a discloser of the Unity of all life. Jeremiah says, *Come, and let us join ourselves to the Lord in a perpetual covenant that shall not be forgotten.* The sacrifice and covenant announce a surrender of the lower nature, which feels itself to be separated from Spirit, to the higher nature, which is forever being One with God. Troward points out that as this Divine At-one-ment is consciously recognized, we come into the knowledge that the Divine Mind is Life in Itself, the very Essence of Being.

It is the recognition of our life as being forever One with God which results in what Jesus meant when he said, *I am come that they might have life, and that they might have it more abundantly.* This would have to be the case if the Law is something which reacts mechanically to our thought. If our patterns of thought arise from a consciousness of our Unity with Good, then in whatever direction they turn we shall be reflecting this Unity of Good. If our thought is rooted in Beauty our acts will be beautiful; if we have a consciousness that Love is at the base of everything, we shall not only love but we shall be loved. Thus we have not destroyed the Law, but have sacrificed the lower to the higher, and in doing so we have made a perpetual covenant with the Eternal. Job says, *Acquaint now thyself with him and be at peace: thereby good shall come unto thee . . . For then shalt thou have thy delight in the Almighty, and shalt lift up thy face unto God.* The Koran states the same truth when it says, *But God will increase the guidance of the already guided.* And the Text of Taoism says, *In the way of Heaven there is no partiality of Love; it is always on the side of the good man.*

Troward explains that from this conception of Unity arises the idea of guidance and protection, which he reminds us recurs throughout the Bible under the emblem of the Shepherd and the Sheep. *The Lord is my shepherd; I shall not want . . . I am the good shepherd . . . Give ear, O shepherd of Israel. . . .* Often we fail to be guided by the Good Shepherd, which is the indwelling Christ referred to in Psalm 119:176: *I have gone astray like a lost sheep.* And in Isaiah: *All we like sheep have gone astray; we have turned every one to his own way.* It is only when the higher qualities are guided by the Divine Instinct, which is the Christ-Mind within us, that we have discovered true Guidance.

Troward tells us that just as Israel represented the attitude of the Shepherd and the Sheep, so Egypt represented a principle of disunion with Good. Genesis 46:34: *. . . every shepherd is an abomination unto the Egyptians.* What is this but a veiled statement referring to man's lack of the knowledge of Divine Guidance, or desire for it?

This Divine Guidance must be found in Universal Mind, and Troward is careful to point out that such Guidance is impossible unless the individual mind first recognizes the Universal Mind as an Intelligence capable of giving the highest instruction. Why, we might ask, does not Universal Mind impose this knowledge upon us willy-nilly? And the answer again takes us back to the starting point of all philosophic discussion relative to the freedom of man. Ecclesiastes says, *Lo, this only have I found, that God hath made man upright; but they have sought out many inventions.* Here is a clear statement that even the Divine Creative Wisdom cannot impose full-fledged individuality, but that such individuality must be left alone to discover itself.

From the teachings of Hermes we read: *But the All Father Mind being Life and Light did bring forth Man coequal to Himself.* And in the Koran: *You created man and You know what his soul whispereth to him, and You are closer to him than his neck vein.* And from Fragments of a Faith Forgotten: *Thou hast begotten Man in Thy self-born Mind, and in Thy reflection . . . he is the man begotten of Mind . . . Thou hast given all things to the Man.* In the Chaldean Oracles we find these words: *The Father of man and gods placed Mind in Soul and Soul in inert Body.* Again in St. John 1:5: *And the light shineth in darkness, and the darkness comprehended it not.* The Text of Taoism asks why the darkness comprehended it not when it says, *But how can the Tao be so obscure that there should be a true and a false in It . . . Tao becomes obscured through the small comprehension.* Surely this means that perfection already exists but we do not realize it.

We find Christ described as the Good Shepherd who giveth his life for his sheep. This could not mean the actual giving of life, since Life is that which cannot be either taken or given. To give life would be to suppose death. The Bible clearly states that man is the author of the idea of death and of resurrection: *For as in Adam all die, even so in Christ shall all be made alive.* It is evident death refers not to an actual cessation of existence or to the destruction of Being, but rather the transmutation of the lower into the higher. Troward tells us that Jesus stands before us as the Grand Master of Mental Science.

The Great Sacrifice which Jesus made was what Troward calls The Great Suggestion. That is, the entire mission of Jesus points to the necessity of Divine Guidance through our conscious cooperation with the Supreme Spirit. It was his mission

THE GREAT WAYSHOWER

to become the Wayshower. He said, *I am the way, the truth, and the life; no man cometh unto the Father but by me.* He was referring to the Universal *I AM* individualized in each one of us as the individualized *I.* The two are One.

It was the purpose of Jesus to reveal the Self to the self, or as an ancient scripture says, *to raise the self by the Self.* He told his disciples: *God is not the God of the dead, but of the living.* God, being the very Life Principle, does not perceive death. There is no death. It is evident that Jesus as the Wayshower was not trying to show the way from death into life, but rather from one state of existence into another; from a lower to a higher plane.

We read in the Zend-Avesta: *If death come at eve, may healing come at daybreak. Let showers shower down new waters, new earth, new trees, new health, and new healing powers.* What does this mean other than that the higher shall govern the lower; evil shall give way to Good; the beneficence of the outpouring of the Spirit shall fill the upturned bowl of acceptance from Its universal horn of plenty. *The eternal God is thy refuge, and underneath are the everlasting arms. . . .* (Deuteronomy 33:27). Job said, *Yea, surely God will not do wickedly, neither will the Almighty pervert judgment.* And in Psalm 19:7-8: *The law of the Lord is perfect, converting the soul . . . The statutes of the Lord are right, rejoicing the heart: the commandment of the Lord is sure, enlightening the eyes.* From the Chaldean Oracles: *For the Self begotten One, the Father Mind, perceiving His own Works sowed into all . . . so that all might continue living on for endless time. And that . . . the Father's Light might never fail.*

The great mission of Jesus was not to convert death into life nor to transmute a material universe into a spiritual one, for either of these propositions would be impossible. He plainly told his disciples that God is not the author of death; that God, being the spiritual Principle of Life, cannot conceive death. Therefore there are no dead men. He also told them to look about them and rightly estimate the universe in which they lived, which they thought to be separated from pure Spirit. *Behold, the kingdom of God is within you.*

Varying degrees of intellectual and spiritual comprehension automatically divide people into different levels of consciousness, from which levels each must interpret Life as he sees It. Kipling says, *And each, in his separate star, shall draw the Thing as he sees It, for the God of Things as They are.* We must interpret the mission of Jesus from the viewpoint of a Supreme Being who consciously sacrificed the Beloved Son in atonement for the sins of the world, or else we must believe that the Beloved Son himself offered the sacrifice, not as a propitiation to the Universal Creative Spirit but as an example to man. This latter viewpoint seems the more intelligent one. But if an individual has not yet reached a spiritual perspective where he recognizes the true significance of sacrificing the lower nature to the higher, there is still a great lesson in the act of Jesus delivering his human life to the needs of those whose philosophy is one of materialism.

Thus the sacrifice of Jesus is designed to meet the need of all classes. The human body sacrificed on the cross symbolizes the union of God with man, of heaven with earth. It is surrendering the lower to the higher nature, the lesser to the greater. The *not-being* is sacrificed to *Being*.

It is never enough, however, to leave principles strung on symbolic meanings. Unless our Bible, like other bibles of the world, delivers a message which is practical as well as idealistic, then it is of little value to us while we live in this world. But Troward tells us that the Bible is the Book of the Emancipation of Man. It teaches a Principle which we can demonstrate in our individual experience. Assuming the creative power of thought, it tells us in many ways how to use this creative power constructively and how to avoid using it destructively.

Moses the Lawgiver taught an immutable Law of Cause and Effect; Jesus the Wayshower, without denying the Mosaic Law, told us that we must add Love to the Law. In these two great central figures of the Bible we find a clear, comprehensive teaching of the nature of the Universe and the relationship between the Creative Spirit and ourselves. Moses proclaimed this relationship to be one of absolute, mathematical, cold, unfailing Cause and Effect. There is something that grinds out every act to its logical conclusion. This same law Buddha clearly taught. Moses, looking down the corridors of time and peering into the future, declared that God would raise up another prophet like unto him. He perceived either by logical deduction or through intuition that his teachings would not be complete until some personal element had been added to his concept of the Law of Cause and Effect.

Science has proved the universe in action to be a mechanical force, but does not disprove a spontaneous Presence in addition to the mechanical force. A modern scientist has inferred that we think of the universe in terms of an Infinite Thinker thinking mathematically, meaning that we may think of the universe as a dual unity of spontaneous self-knowingness and reactive self-manifesting law. Here we have the Infinite Thinker and the mathematical thought. We have both an engine and an engineer. We have a universe not only of law and order, but also of feeling, love, consciousness, truth, and beauty.

Science observes a mechanical universe because it studies the universe in action. Whether we study physical or mechanical laws or the movement of thought, we shall always find a mechanical movement. However, it does not seem intelligent to leave out the Thinker. The artist is superior to his art; the engineer controls his engine. One of our great scientists tells us that science has not discovered anything which denies a Universal Consciousness in which the relationship of the Supreme Creative Spirit is to us as a parent to its offspring.

So we find that the mission of Jesus was to complete the Law of Moses. He explained that he came not to destroy but to fulfill. He breathed beauty, warmth, and color into life, and thus the very Law which had produced bondage, by the divine alchemy of his creative touch, was transmuted into freedom.

BELIEF, FAITH, and PRAYER

And the prayer of faith shall save the sick, and the Lord shall raise him up (James 5:15). What then, is the prayer of faith?

Jesus clearly taught that Spiritual Power works through man at the level of his belief, implying that it would work as he believed and while he believed. He ascribed a mighty power to belief and to faith, and we find that throughout the ages faith has been honored. Most certainly some people's prayers have been answered, but not all persons' prayers have been answered in the way in which they wished them to be answered.

How are we going to account for the fact that one person's prayers are answered and another's are not? Must we admit that there are degrees in which prayers are answered? And if so, why? Is one man's faith better than another's? Is God more pleased with one man's petition than another's?

It seems a pretty tough problem, until we understand what Jesus meant when he said, *Go thy way, and as thou hast believed, so be it done unto thee.*

What did he imply? He implied that it is done unto us by some impersonal Principle, a Principle which knows neither Jew nor Gentile, but knows only Its own ability to do. It will do as quickly for one as for another. The Law is no respecter of persons but works alike for each and all.

Jesus not only said, *So be it done unto thee.* He said, *As thou hast believed.* The impersonal Law, which is the actor, does it unto us, but only as we believe. Immediately we recognize our old friend the Law of Cause and Effect. It is done unto us as we believe, and if we can believe only a little, then only what we call a little is done. But if we believe in what the consensus of human opinion has called a lot, then a lot is done. Not that there is a big or little in the Truth, but that we measure it. Well did the Great Teacher say, *With what measure ye mete, it shall be measured to you again.* It is done unto us, but only as we believe.

What is belief? Most surely belief is a certain way of thinking; it is an activity of consciousness. Belief is a thing of thought, and being a thing of thought we can change belief. And if what a man believes decides what is going to happen to him, the most important thing for him to do is regulate his belief so that what happens will be good for him, and he will be glad to have it happen, and joyously welcome it.

What is most likely to change our belief from a negative to a positive viewpoint? What thought, what hope, what expression, what stimulus is most likely to change our belief? This Jesus established in the Sermon on the Mount when he said that the meek shall inherit the earth; that the peacemakers shall be called the children of God. In other statements he showed us how to reform our belief so that it could partake of the nature of Reality and would contain within itself everything necessary for our well-being. This is also what the Apostle meant when he said that we should think on whatsoever things are good, true, and beautiful.

Faith is an affirmative mode of thought. Faith says, "I can, " rather than "I cannot" or "I shall not." We can learn to have faith in abundance rather than in poverty. We can change our thought in regard to lack. This is what treatment is for. Instead of saying, "There is not enough good to go around," we say, "All the power there is, is devoted to my good. I am not afraid of poverty because all the power there is, is devoted to giving me abundance. God provides me with every good thing today, every day, always." Such statements as these will change our belief from denial to one of positive faith. Whatever we can have faith in, and having faith in, can understand, we may experience according to the Law of Cause and Effect. This Law is immutable, invariable, unassailable, and absolute.

"But," someone might ask, "is faith in lack equal to faith in abundance?" The answer to this question is that there is neither lack nor abundance, as such; there is merely what is and the way it works. We are so constituted that faith in love overcomes the belief in hate. Our nature is such that faith in life destroys our fear of death. Our nature is such that faith routs all fear all along the line. The great affirmations of life must, of necessity, destroy their apparent opposites. Nevertheless we cannot overlook the fact that all statements are positive, all statements are affirmations, since each is a statement of one's belief in something.

Right here is where prayer comes in, and of course we are thinking of prayer in its broadest connotation and its most realistic meaning. We are thinking of prayer as the communion of the soul with the Oversoul, with the Divine Creative Presence which is not only in the soul but which *is* the soul. It is more than an individualization; it is also a Universality.

Prayer in its truest sense is not a petition, not a supplication, not a wail of despair; it is rather an alignment, a unifying process which takes place in the mind as it reaches to its Divine Self and to that Power which is greater than human understanding. In the act of such prayerful and reverent communion with God one senses the Unity of Good, the completeness of Life, and at times the veil of doubt is lifted and the face of Reality appears. This consciousness, which has been referred to as the Secret Place of the Most High, is an experience rising out of the conviction that God is all there is, beside Whom there is none else.

Prayer, then, is communion, and this communion pronounces life to be Good. Prayerful communion ascends to that place where unity has not yet become variety, where the unformed One is ready to take any specific shape. In this act of communion the individual becomes copartner with the Eternal and gives birth to time, space, and conditions.

But what could Jesus have meant when he referred to fasting in connection with prayer? It seems evident that he was not necessarily referring to a physical fact, for one of the accusations laid against him was that he drank wine with sinners. He was also accused of breaking the Sabbath by permitting his disciples to pluck corn on the Sabbath day. In fact he seemed to disregard many of the outward forms which were common in his day. He referred to some deeper Principle which physical fasting was intended to symbolize.

This is what he meant when he said that it was not sufficient to make the outside of the platter clean, and again when he said, *Not every one that saith unto me, Lord, Lord, shall enter into the kingdom of heaven.* Perhaps by fasting and prayer Jesus meant such a complete consecration to the ideal that the Creative Genius of the Universe passed immediately into Self-expression through man's imagination.

Such a high altitude of thought could not be described other than by using the symbol of fasting and prayer, and possibly that is why Jesus used it. Suppose we call fasting a determination to refuse further contemplation of the negative. This would be passing from death into life, from negation into affirmation, from denial into acceptance. In this transformation of thought through faith and belief the communion of the soul with its Source would become a pronouncement rather than a petition. This is the position which the enlightened of all ages have taken.

If a person feels that the act of physical fasting is necessary to the consummation of such a devout communion, let him fast, and no person should be so rash as to deny him this privilege. If, on the other hand, he feels that he is not fighting his way but singing a song, let no one deny him the joyous pathway to freedom. For sooner or later all must discover that it is neither fasting nor feasting, but belief, faith, and acceptance which cause one to transcend the lesser good and ascend into that holy mount within where the eye views the world *as one vast plain and one boundless reach of sky.*

We must never forget to make a practical application of this science. In our philosophy it is not enough merely to state a principle. We must apply such a principle to our everyday living, and wherever a need appears we must meet it, not by accepting the inevitability of such a need but by affirming its exact opposite. The need is met when we no longer recognize it as a need but seeing through it envision that Principle which could just as easily remold the need into an acceptance of good. Therefore we are told to think on whatsoever things are true, lovely, and of good report; we should dwell on these things rather than on their apparent opposites.

To put this into practice should be the desire of every sincere seeker after spiritual truth. He must come to believe that there is such a Divine Power waiting his use. He must fully understand that he is the one who knows how to use It and then he must proceed definitely to make use of this Power which is within all men. In actual practice one's life should become a continuous communion with Good.

One's mind should be continuously acknowledging the presence of Good and the Power of Good in one's experience. A practitioner should acknowledge the Power and Presence of this Good in the experience of the one he seeks to help. For the acknowledgment of Good is a creative act making possible its manifestation in human experience. We should *fast* from the idea of lack and *feast* with the idea of plenty. We should *fast* from the idea of poverty and *feast* upon the belief in wealth, and most surely we should abstain from contemplating uncertainties and enter into a long and eternal period of feasting upon certainty. And when the world cries, "Whither goest thou?" something within us should answer, "We know in whom we have believed."

At first this fasting and feasting, this prayer and communion may seem a little difficult. We all are more or less surrounded by negation and this is where the office of prayer enters. It establishes a serenity within the soul enabling it to have confidence in that spirit of acceptance without which the Divine gift is never complete. For how can the Divine gift become complete until one accepts it? There is no song without a singer. And so we must learn joyfully to enter into our Divine inheritance.

What does all this mean other than that we should learn to have confidence in Life, to believe in the Eternal Goodness, and to accept the Divine Bounty? This transformation of thought from negation to affirmation is seldom instantaneous, so one must maintain a flexibility of thought, being willing to bend somewhat before the storms of life but refusing to break. One's thought should have an elasticity which permits it to spring back into place, but it cannot do so unless it is first fully convinced that it does know in Whom it has believed, unless it is completely convinced that the Universe is a spiritual system governed by a Beneficent Consciousness.

This greater vision seldom transpires in one flash of consciousness, although it may do so. More often than not the ascent from our valley of negation to the mountain top of realization is slow. But each step on the road entices us with the enchantment of a new vista, and, judging from past experiences and former transformations, the pathway upon which we travel leads to the summit and we press on with joy.

By some Divine interior awareness, call it what we will, there is an intuition within man which pushes him forward. There is some spark which has never been entirely extinguished. The prayer of faith and belief, communion of the soul with its Source, fans this spark into a Divine blaze in whose light dark shadows no longer lurk. This is inspiration. This is illumination. This is the perception of wholeness.

Suppose a man were to prepare himself a mental diet garnished with spiritual realization, his meat the living word, his bread manna from heaven, his fruit the inspiration of hope, and his wine the essence of joy. And suppose in addition to this he should see this table spread before him in the wilderness and waited upon by the Law, the servent of God and man, would he not then realize that he is to-day in the Kingdom of Heaven, that today God is his Host, and would he not exclaim, "Oh, Wilderness were Paradise enow!"

BIBLES OF THE WORLD

*Fragments from the spiritual history of the race revealing
the fundamental Unity of religious thought and experience.*

BUDDHISM

Be not concerned with other men's evil works or deeds or neglect of good. Look rather to thine own sins and negligence.

Though one should conquer in battle thousands and thousands of men, whoso shall conquer himself — he is the greatest of warriors. To overcome oneself is better truly than to overcome others.

CHRISTIANITY

Thou hypocrite, first cast out the beam out of thine own eye; and then shalt thou see clearly to cast out the mote out of thy brother's eye.

Wherefore let him that thinketh he standeth take heed lest he fall.

CONFUCIANISM

The good in you I will not dare to keep concealed. And for the evil in me I will not dare to forgive myself. I will examine these things in harmony with the mind of God.

Give repose to your mind. Examine your virtue. Send far forward your plans. And thus by your generous forbearance you will make people repose in what is good.

HINDUISM

The man of steady wisdom, having subdued all senses, becomes fixed in Me, the Supreme. His wisdom is well established.

To those men, ever controlled, who think on Me and worship Me with undivided hearts, I bring the power to gain and guard.

ZOROASTRIANISM

May thy mind be master of its vow!
May thy soul be master of its vow!
And all the nights of thy life
Mayest thou live on in the joy of thy soul!

JAINISM

Prove constant to truth.

Right belief depends on the acquaintance with truth, or the devotion to those who know the truth.

Exert yourself in the truth. Knowing the truth, one should live up to it.

LESSON 6

MIND

How the Mind Creates

A Message from Ernest Holmes

You will find several references in this lesson to cross sections from our Textbook. They are of vital importance so please read them carefully. For what you are trying to discover is perhaps the greatest of all truths, which is that there is only One Mind in the Universe and you use It.

You and I do not have a mind separate from God any more than we have a law of nature that belongs to us individually. Here we are in the midst of nature and we can learn how to use her laws because the Mind of God is in us, telling us about these laws and how to use them. This is true of every scientific discovery, and none the less true in the discovery of the Science of Mind and how to use it, for it is both an exact and an exacting science.

As our lesson says, we all use this Mind and live in this Divine Presence. Each individualizes It. God, the Divine Presence, is personal to you, and the Law of Mind is right where you are, ready to be used. It cannot refuse your approach because It is a Law.

In the article on The Consciousness That Heals *we are trying more strongly to emphasize that there is a scientific method, a right way to use the Laws of Mind. The article on* Religion *deals with Spiritual Consciousness, and shows the fundamental mental attitudes that we should assume.*

You will realize that we do not criticize anyone's religion because we believe in all religions. We are trying to arrive at the essence of all religions, for when we strip them of nonessentials they all teach the same thing. This is why we are enclosing quotations from different religions of the world.

MIND

How the Mind Creates

(textbook reference: pages 87-92)

One of the most difficult things for us to realize is that there is but One Mind in the Universe. We are accustomed to think of our individual minds and the Mind of God as though they were separate and divided from each other, and yet in reality there is but One Mind which we all use.

If you turn to page 41 under the heading *A Riddle of Simplicity,* and read through to the bottom of page 42, you will get a better understanding of the reality of this Unity of Mind. You will notice at the bottom of page 41 these words: *The intelligence by and through which we perceive that there is a Spiritual Presence and an Infinite Mind . . . constitutes our receptivity to It.* That is, the very act of self-knowing which takes place in your thought is in reality this One Mind recognizing Itself.

As much of this One Mind is released through us into operation as we are able to embody. The action of this Mind through our thought creates the forms which appear in our experience. This should be kept in mind while reading on page 483, *The Law of Correspondents.* Each one of us is a law unto himself through his particular use of the Creative Law of the Universe.

We need not seek other powers or other minds, but we must clearly perceive that all the power there is has already been delivered unto us. All the Good there is, is ours, but we must consciously enter into this Good. If we have not been experiencing as much Good as we desire we must make definite and conscious use of the Law with the direct end in mind of experiencing more Good. We must really use our technique for conscious practice.

On page 458 you will find a description of a concrete method of practice under the heading *A Formula for Effective Prayer*. Jesus told us that when we pray we are to believe that we have already received. This is not always easy, and yet the greatest spiritual genius who ever lived gave us this formula, this method of approach, this conscious use of the Law of Spiritual Cause and Effect.

When we pray we must believe that we already possess the object of our desire. This calls for implicit trust; for complete faith. Until we believe that we already possess it, we have not created the image of our desire and projected it into the Creative Medium so that it may attract to itself that which shall give it form.

We should believe that God wills everything Good for us; that it would be impossible for God to will anything other than Good. We should think of the Law as our obedient servant and the Spirit as our immediate friend. The Spirit ever inspires us, the Law ever obeys us.

This formula for prayer which Jesus laid down for our use certainly reaches the very rock-bottom of Spiritual Causation. *Blessed are they that have not seen, and yet have believed.* For when we turn from the confusion of fear to the certainty of faith, we may be sure that the Universal will respond and that we shall demonstrate our desired Good.

On page 88, the third paragraph, we are told that *the Body of the Universe is the result of the thought of Spirit operating through the medium of Soul.* You will find on page 633 a definition of the word *Soul* as we use it. The Soul represents the Creative Medium, the Universal Law, which is subject both to the Will of God and to the will of man.

Soul has been spoken of as the servant of the Spirit throughout the ages. Soul is Subjective Law. It has been referred to as the Womb of Nature because it has been thought of as the Feminine Principle of nature, which means the productive side, that Creative Medium which receives the images of thought, whether of God or of man, and gives birth to corresponding form.

Under the heading *The "Personalness" of God* (page 88), let us carefully consider that Spirit is more than an abstract principle. It must forever be to each one of us warm, colorful, but Infinite Personalness. As we read in the Glossary on page 618, under *Personalness: To think of God simply as an Infinite Principle would be to resolve the Divine Being into an Infinite It.* The text states, also, that God is personal to all who believe in Him.

Let us carefully consider once more the dual unity of Spirit and Law, and though we may seem to be continually referring to this topic, it tends to make us realize the necessity of coming to see definitely, and having it fixed completely in our minds, that there is a difference between Person and Principle. In working out Universal Principles we need never deny Universal Personalness.

We may and should retain all of the warmth and color, all of the responsiveness latent in the idea of Personalness. We need this if we are to have a true sense of our right relationship to the Spirit. I think this is an important thing for us to consider and we should give it a great deal of thought.

Read the Meditation on page 548 called *The Personality of God,* and also the Meditation on page 549, *Unity.* After having read these meditations, combining the two as one, think carefully on the meaning of each word and phrase. Do this daily until finally there comes to you, as there will come, a sense of your unity with the Whole. You will discover an intimate relationship with the Universe which will enable you to use It even more effectively for definite purposes.

The question which so many people ask, in taking up the study of a metaphysical system of thought, is whether in so doing they will lose God. As a matter of fact, for the first time they will find the Real Divine. On page 419, the third paragraph, you will read that all the mystics have recognized the unity of God and man. We can never be separated from that life of pure Spirit of which we are some part. Always this Essence is flowing into action through the imagination and the will. The Essence, the imagination, and the will are spontaneous, the action is mechanical.

Read page 447, *How to Approach the Spirit.* You will see that the consciousness of the Divine Presence is an inner experience. It would be very difficult, and perhaps impossible, to give any dogmatic instructions or method of procedure which would be sure to enable us to become conscious of this inner Spirit. The Spirit is already here, and we must feel for It until we really feel It, or, as the mystic said, *Act as though I am and I will be.* We should daily practice this Presence of God.

MIND

In the first paragraph on page 91 we are told that the Soul, or the Subjective Medium, executes the will of the Spirit but has no self-choice. It merely reflects the images that the conscious Spirit holds before It or casts into It. This Principle that we have to demonstrate — that all objective form starts in a subjective idea — is the foundation of scientific mental work. As a practitioner you must use this Principle with deliberate intent and with specific purpose.

On page 435 we are told to pray believing; that prayer should be direct and specific, and should always be accompanied by positive recognition and receptivity. You will soon discover that mental and spiritual work is definite. When you give a treatment you know exactly what you are doing. There is never anything indefinite or vague about it.

A treatment is an active thing; this activity is mental recognition, and such mental recognition is usually put into the form of spoken words followed by a deep inner realization of the truth of those words. You will find the process simple and direct.

On page 415, the second paragraph, is the statement that we must realize our Divine Partnership, a partnership which exists between the visible world of effects and the invisible world of Causation. Man's place in the creative order is really that of a distributor of the Divine gifts. He uses the Law, which already exists, and gives form to the Substance, which already exists, and he does this because the impulsion of the Originating Spirit, the Parent Mind, is already operating through his imagination and will.

Our paragraph says, *The hope of destiny is latent in the slumbering thought and genius lies buried until the attention is winged with love and reason.* The impulsion of Love, the sense of our Divine relationship to God and to each other, the resulting compassionate desire to help others, is the awakening of the soul to the high call of the Spirit. But since everything in the Universe is reasonable, we shall never be called upon to do anything that contradicts an intelligent, law-abiding Universe.

In giving your treatments you should always feel the Divine Presence, but you should never forget the immutable Law. For in such degree as your word is in harmony with Truth, it must be Power. Thus the Will of God is made manifest through the Law of Life, which returns to us exactly what we reflect into It.

We should ponder the deep meaning of this rather abstract but at the same time simple concept of the Universe — that Universal Laws are always Self-Active. This means that when it comes to giving a treatment, what you put into your treatment, as consciousness, will appear in physical form. Not only will it appear, but it must appear.

We are ready, then, to consider the main paragraph on page 92, which is the description of the creative and reflective Law of Spirit. The Law says *Yes* when you say *Yes* and *No* when you say *No*. If you hold a triangle before a mirror, the image of the triangle is reflected in it. Just so, if you think poverty into the Law It reflects poverty back to you. It reflects fear for fear, faith for faith.

But because this Law reflects the exact image of thought that we think into It, and has no other choice in the matter, then it follows that no matter what the Law may be holding now as being true about us, through a new process of thinking we so completely change Its tendency as to alter the experience. If this were not true it would be useless for us to pursue these studies in the Science of Mind, but our study of this Principle will enable us through practice to prove that the Principle is correct.

On page 339, second paragraph, you will find a discussion of involution and evolution, the Law of Cause and Effect. Please note that evolution is the effect of Intelligence and not Its cause, and that evolution follows involution. At the same time read the definition of *Evolution* on page 590, and *Involution* on page 603. Try in your imagination to see exactly how this works. Try to sense that the entire process of evolution, which is the passing of Spirit into form, is an effect of thought; that your entire experience is an effect, and that you stand in the position of the conscious creator of that effect.

Therefore learn definitely and deliberately to create new images of thought that new and better conditions may be cast in the mold of your experience.

SUMMARY

There is only One Mind and you use It. The individual mind is a center in this Mind and not separate from It. God wills only that which is Good for us, but our thought is creative and automatically brings to us the things we think about.

The Spirit is more than an abstract principle. It is a warm, living, colorful Presence personal to each one.

God can have no will for anyone other than the Will of Good, freedom, liberty, life, truth, love, and beauty.

The Spirit is at the center of your own being; if you believe It will reveal Itself to you, It will.

Spiritual mind treatment is always an active thing. It is the Law of Mind in Action. It is Mind doing something definite as It reacts to our thought.

A consciousness of Love and of the Divine Presence is the foundation for all use of the Law of Mind. We feel this Presence and we use this Law.

No matter what happened yesterday, we can change it today because the Law reflects the images of our thoughts as we think them.

Because we can wipe out the old images of thought or their effects and create new ones, we are free. But even this freedom will do us no good unless we use it. Therefore we must definitely use the Law of Good at all times and for all purposes. Each must become the arbiter of his fate, and learn to mold his future more nearly after his heart's desire.

QUESTIONS

Brief answers to these questions should be written out by the student after studying this lesson, and the answers compared with those in the Appendix.

1. What is it within us that knows?

2. To what extent can we use the Mind of God?

3. What do we mean by being conscious of and embodying the Mind of God?

4. How much power and good do we have to use?

5. How do we make prayer effective?

6. What is the will of God for us?

7. How should we think of Spirit and the Law?

8. Is the Spirit personal to us?

9. Is the Law personal to us?

10. What is the difference between Spirit as Person, and Law as Principle?

11. In dealing with God as Infinite Mind, do we lose anything?

12. Is mental work a definite thing?

13. What is man's place in the creative order of the Universe?

14. What gives power to our word?

15. How can we use the Law of Cause and Effect as a principle of freedom rather than bondage?

METAPHYSICAL INTERPRETATIONS OF THE BIBLE

based on

Thomas Troward's *Bible Mystery and Bible Meaning*

THE TEMPLE OF TRUTH

In his chapter on *The Building of the Temple,* Troward says that the Bible teaches that certain universal principles are at the root of everything, whether it be the world of man or the Divine World. God, man, and the Universe all have fundamental laws unifying and coordinating the inner relationship of the parts with the Whole. In this way each plane reproduces the one just below it on a higher level, and the one just above it on a lower level; the same laws obtain on all planes, or as Hermes said, *As above, so below.*

It was a realization that man in his real nature reflects or reproduces the Universal Spirit that caused Jesus to say, *Be ye therefore perfect, even as your Father which is in heaven is perfect.* And John to say, *Beloved, now are we the sons of God, and it doth not yet appear what we shall be: but we know that, when he shall appear, we shall be like him; for we shall see him as he is.*

The Bible, in its many and varied illustrations, points to three central themes, God, Man, and the Universe. Troward states: *However deep the mysteries we may encounter, there is nothing unnatural anywhere. Everything has its place in the true order of the Great Whole.* Ignorance of the true order will not exempt us from suffering the results of a misuse of its laws; hence ignorance binds us until we become redeemed by the Truth. This is the meaning of sin and salvation. Since sin means making a mistake or missing the mark, salvation must stand for the correction of the mistake or hitting the mark. Both sin and salvation are potential in all of us since we are individuals.

The laws of nature never change, and Troward tells us: *The only question is whether through our ignorance we shall use them in that inverted sense which sums them all up in the Law of Death, or in that true and harmonious order which sums them up in the Law of Life.* He also points out that Solomon's Temple symbolizes this Grand Order of the Universe. Before the Temple stood two pillars, Jachin

CHANGE YOUR THINKING, CHANGE YOUR LIFE 157

and Boaz. These pillars were in no way connected with Temple. Jachin stands for *The One*, while Boaz stands for *The Voice* or *The Word*. Jachin, then, stands for the mathematical principle in the Universe, and Boaz for the Word which utilizes this principle, or as Troward said, *The formulated Word is the expression of a definite Purpose and therefore stands for the action of Intelligent Volition.* He adds that we enter the Temple only by passing between these two pillars which symbolize the combined action of Law and Volition. It is one of the purposes of the Bible, Troward states, to teach us how to pass between these two pillars and into the Temple that inner secrets of the sanctuary may be open to us.

The Temple refers to man's mind, consciousness, or being. *Know ye not that ye are the temple of God, and that the Spirit of God dwelleth in you? . . . the temple of God is holy, which temple ye are.* Emerson said, *God builds his Temple in the heart on the ruins of churches and religions.* And Seneca affirmed, *Temples are not to be built for God with stones piled on high; He is to be consecrated in the breast of each.* St. Augustine wrote, *A pure mind is a holy temple of God, and a clean heart without sin is His best altar.*

Troward explains that Moses, Solomon, and Jesus are the three chief characters of the Bible, and that they are all builders of the Temple. His comparison of these three men is unique and interesting. He tells us: *Moses erected the tabernacle, that portable temple which accompanied the Israelites in their journeyings.* It is evident that this tabernacle stands for an external and temporary representation of the Divine Creative Spirit. It is symbolic of the human body. In II Corinthians 5:1-2 we read: *For we know that if our earthly house of this tabernacle were dissolved, we have a building of God, a house not made with hands, eternal in the heavens. For in this we groan, earnestly desiring to be clothed upon with our house which is from heaven.* Does this not mean that the human body has a Divine Pattern in Heaven, a Spiritual Prototype? Since Jesus described Heaven as an interior state, we know that we are to be clothed upon, not by some force or power external to the Self, but by some creative agency already within the Self. Thus the tabernacle of Moses was called *the antitype of the True or Heavenly.*

Troward tells us, *Solomon reproduced it (Moses' tabernacle) in an ediface of wood and stone fixed firmly upon its rocky foundation.* Jesus, with a still deeper insight, perceived a Temple that could not decay — *Destroy this temple, and in three days I will raise it up.* Troward states that the three builders, each in his own way, proclaim the same all-embracing truth that God, Man, and the Universe, however varied may be the multiplicity of outward forms, are One. A conscious knowledge of this Divine Unity is the key which unlocks the Temple door through which we pass to the Secret Place of the Most High.

The building of the Temple is something which takes place through interior perception, through a recognition of one's true relationship with the Universal Wholeness. Not that man awakes to a recognition of the Universal Wholeness to the exclusion of his individual being, but that he as an individual is immersed in pure Spirit; he is an individualized *I* within the *I AM,* recognizing his greater Self to be the Universal Wholeness. It is this greater Self that Troward points out to us as the true Builder, because it is none other than the reproduction of the Infinite Creative Power of the Universe. It is the recognition that the Spirit of God is also the Spirit of man, bringing us again to Emerson's concept of *One Mind common to all individual men.*

Troward wishes us to realize that the key to a proper understanding of the scriptures is a realization that the Universal cannot, as such, initiate a course of action on the plane of the particular. Now this is not as difficult to understand as it appears to be. It means this: God can give us only what we take; what God does for us He must do through us. If we are to reproduce the Mind of God it can be done only by the Mind of God incarnating Itself in us. This is the only way that the apparent two can become One.

It is this Unity with Life at the very root of our being which makes our thought creative. Thought is creative not by will, wishing, longing, prayer, or supplication, but because it is its nature to be so. Man is a microcosm within the Macrocosm, a little world within the Big World. But because man is an individualized expression of God-Consciousness he has the prerogative of apparent isolation. He must consciously enter the Temple; he must come into conscious union with the Spirit which indwells his soul. This is the Secret Place of the Most High, that brings him under the shadow of the Almighty. That is, it brings him under the government of Good. And according to the Law of Cause and Effect, it is only when he recognizes his union with the First Cause that he can consciously partake of the harvest of such a union.

THE TEMPLE OF TRUTH

Since *harvest* symbolizes a gathering in of the fruits of wisdom, it follows that man with true wisdom must consciously unite himself with Good before he can become a conscious builder of the Temple. Troward tells us that when we enter this Temple a Divine Interpreter will meet us on the threshold. *Threshold* is described as a symbol of higher planes of Mind which are the entrance to Spirit. Thus we see that being met on the threshold means entering into a conscious union with Reality.

Each individual is a Temple in himself. Within this Temple before the altar stand the high priest of the mind and the priest of speech. Before the altar stands the Mind which perceives and the Law which executes. The true priest is one who knows there is no gulf between God and man; that the Divine is forever pouring out Its beneficence. It is the business of the priest to become the mediator between this inward Principle and Its outward manifestation. It is written that there is no mediator save Christ, which means that there is no mediator save our own true nature.

No one can enter the Temple for us but ourselves. No one can offer the sacrifice but ourselves. No one can receive the blessing but ourselves. Thus ancient wisdom tells us that the altar, the sacrifice, the one who makes the sacrifice, and the one to whom it is made, are identical.

It was the same perception of Unity which Whitman disclosed in his great poem to himself. It is only when a person recognizes that each must become his own priest that he truly stands before the altar; it is only when he has renounced all disunion that the proper sacrifice has been made, and it is only when this has been done in Love that the sacrifice is acceptable. Thus one greater than Moses said that it is useless to lay our gift upon the altar while we have anything against our fellow man. This does not mean that God becomes angry with us; it is an affirmation of the Law of Cause and Effect. We can enter into the Nature of Reality only by first complying with such Nature. The giving up of everything which denies this Nature is the great sacrifice.

We must, as Troward suggests, give up everything that denies the creative power of thought; everything that finds itself bound only to external appearances, and everything that denies the fundamental Unity of Good. If we wish to enter into a less limited experience we must sacrifice our limitations. If we wish greater

THE TEMPLE OF TRUTH

Love we must sacrifice our hate. It is impossible to do this, Troward points out, while we persist in the belief that the truly originating causes of things are to be found anywhere but in our own mental attitude.

Again he states that we cannot do this unless we come to realize First Cause as that which acts independently of all conditions. It is self-evident that if we are dealing with Causation we are dealing with that which creates conditions and could not be limited by them. But because our images of thought are too often the mere reflections of our external environment, we automatically limit the gift of Spirit. Consciously we say that since we have never experienced very much happiness we probably never shall; unconsciously we affirm that joy and prosperity do not belong to us; unconsciously we create our patterns of thought after those borrowed from others, not realizing that the act of thought is independent, and that conditions flow from thought. Effect reflects cause.

When we learn to receive our visions of Reality as a result of having entered the *temple not made with hands,* then we shall truly become liberated. The tabernacle which Moses erected in the wilderness will have disappeared, the temple made of wood and stone which Solomon built will have crumbled. But the real Temple, the Spiritual Prototype of our external forms, will have become revealed.

What particular lesson are we to learn from this symbolic presentation? For it is certainly never wise to leave things in their symbolic state, at least it would not be practical. The lesson is this: The story of the building of the Temple does not in reality depict some ancient happening, nor yet some far off divine event; it is the story of every man's life as he lives it here and now. What is the dominant suggestion or belief in our consciousness? Are we looking merely at the external? Is our prayer one of the intellect only, or have we passed between the pillars of Jachin and Boaz? Have we understood the meaning of the Law and of the Word, and have we realized that these pillars must be arched by Love and Unity?

If so, we stand on the threshold of a greater Reality. The doorway to the Temple is open and we may advance, not with fear and trembling but with confidence, peace, and perfect trust. Petition has now become transmuted into communion, which is conscious unity with the Divine Creative Spirit. Hate, fear, and uncertainty have been left behind. The gift which we lay upon the altar of our faith is now acceptable because it unifies with Life. Hence our request will be answered.

We would miss the meaning of this chapter if we failed to realize that the true Temple is our own consciousness, and that the consciousness of Good which we entertain is not different from or other than the essence of Goodness Itself. It is not separated from the Power which both creates and projects. Therefore Jesus said that because he always did the Will of God, because he lived in union with the Nature of Reality, his requests were always granted. He was not referring to the nature of a deity who withheld gifts from some while granting them to others, but to Reality Itself, which cannot refuse to deliver Itself when we comply with Its nature. This is the gift made from the foundations of the world.

Our Temple is the Self; our altar the denial of evil and the affirmation of Good; our sacrifice a renouncing of the great negations; our gift, which is acceptable, the supreme affirmation: *I AM that I AM, beside which there is none other*. This Universal *I AM* and this individual *I* are one and indivisible.

THE CONSCIOUSNESS THAT HEALS

In the Fifth Chapter of James we read: *And the prayer of faith shall save the sick, and the Lord shall raise him up.* When we analyze what the prayer of faith means we discover that it is a statement of belief in some power which is able, ready, and willing to do the healing. At first this may seem like a rather cold-blooded analysis, for to pick a prayer of faith apart seems to rob it of its sentimentality. Nevertheless if we would arrive at a state of consciousness that heals we must be willing to analyze some of those things which seem so intimate and so holy that we dislike even to mention them.

The prayer of faith may be thought of as a petition, as a beseeching, or as an agonizing cry of the soul for deliverance, but whatever we term it and from whatever viewpoint we look at it, we discover that it still is an attitude of thought, a way of thinking, a movement in consciousness. If the prayer is one of faith, then this mental movement is one of acceptance, for *faith is an acceptance unqualified by denial.*

Complete faith is absolute and positive. Faith is the attitude of one who makes a complete mental surrender. It can arise only through a consciousness of complete abandonment. To the consciousness of faith there are no longer any arguments against its conviction. Faith has no opposites; it is an uncompromising mental attitude, and this is exactly what the prayer of faith is. It is a prayer, a petition, or a beseeching stated in some form of mental acceptance, unqualified belief, unquestioned trust.

While the burden of petition and the necessity of faith rests on the one making the petition or having the faith, the *response* to this petition and this faith is made by some creative agency which has the power and the willingness to perform the act. It is God who raises him up.

What is this but a statement of *spiritual cause and effect,* for it plainly states that we have our part to play in creative faith, and that as a result of our belief some principle in nature responds by accomplishing the desired result. This result is obtained without further effort on our part. Another parallel statement to this is: *And ye shall know the truth, and the truth shall make you free,* which implies that there is a truth, which known, automatically becomes demonstrated.

Surely in these two statements, *The prayer of faith shall save the sick, and the Lord shall raise him up,* and *Ye shall know the truth, and the truth shall make you free,* a definite principle is involved which all can understand and use. It is the understanding of principles with the ability to make conscious use of them that constitutes what is called the scientific method in any and all research into the secrets of nature.

There are several things which happen in the pursuit of this scientific method. First someone evolves the theory that a certain principle exists in the Universe. Perhaps through observation, possibly by intuition, he conceives his theory. Having conceived this theory he begins to experiment with it, and if his theory is correct he discovers that there are certain laws involved. These laws flow out of his principle, so to speak.

Having discovered his principle he experiments with it until he learns more of the laws which govern it. Next he uses these laws for definite purposes. What has he done? He has uttered what might be called a prayer of faith. He has felt that certain things must be true, and he has had such faith in his belief that he has actually set about to discover the laws governing his theory. If his theory is correct his faith is justified. He uncovers the natural laws of cause and effect relative to that theory. The scientific researcher always finds that there are no variations whatsoever from this result. When he uncovers a principle of nature it is changeless and invariable — he can always depend upon it.

Civilizations may come and go, empires may flourish and decay, time may pass, and change may deface all previous experience, but law is eternal. Thus the scientist learns to depend on law. His prayer of faith to his principle is a willingness to comply with the operation of its law. His cooperation and his understanding teach him how to use this law for specific purposes. We might say his prayer of faith enables him to use the principle intelligently and definitely. Thus his prayer of faith causes a response on the part of the law, and the operation of the law accomplishes the desired result. What is this but another way of saying that the prayer of faith shall save the sick and God shall raise him up?

The two ideas are identical, but because we have been so accustomed to thinking of spiritual things in unnatural ways, and because we have been so used to divorcing natural things from the spiritual, we have believed in a dualistic universe and have failed to realize that Spiritual Causation is in reality the invisible end of every objective fact.

To whom does any principle of nature belong? We have never yet heard of a sane scientific man declaring that the principle of mathematics or chemistry belongs to him because he happens to be of some particular religious conviction.

Science knows no race, no particular generation of men, and no separate dispensation. The only revelation that science knows is that revelation which comes to the listening ear, the expectant thought, the intelligent uncovering of nature's laws. When a scientific principle is uncovered it belongs not to the scientist who uncovered it, but to the God who gave it and to any individual who has sense enough to use it.

Let us take our scientific method and return to the thought that the prayer of faith shall save the sick and the Lord shall raise him up. The prayer of faith is a consciousness of acceptance, a mental conclusion in a person's mind, based on the belief that the Creative Spirit responds directly to him.

In the words of Jesus: *What things soever ye desire when ye pray, believe that ye receive them and ye shall have them.* When we bring the two words *soever* and *them* into bold relief, what do we have? We have what we might call a conscious specializing of the Law for definite purposes. The prayer of faith is a prayer which expresses faith about *some particular* thing. *What things soever* include our specific wants, our definite needs. If a man were praying for a home he would not be asking for an automobile. If he were praying that his neighbor be healed he would not be asking for money with which to take a trip.

When we return to our central thought that the prayer of faith shall save the sick and God shall raise him up, we must remember that the prayer of faith is definite — it is faith *in something* and *about something*. This type of prayer is not generalized, but specific. It is conscious and definite.

This brings it into line with the scientific method, for the scientific use of any law is always conscious and always definite. The principle governing the law is universal, but the use of the law is always individual. It is this element of personality injected into the Universal Law which differentiates it when we use it for specific purposes. The consciousness that heals is definite and deliberate; it is a specializing of the Universal Law. In this Law we may have absolute and implicit confidence, but we must also remember that the Law can do *for* us only what it does *through* us. Its energy and creativeness must be interpreted through our belief and imagination.

We should add another proposition to our general statement, which is: *And as thou hast believed, so be it done unto thee.* We now have these words — *what things soever, them,* and *as.* This is but another way of saying that if we want the principle of electricity to light our living room we must provide a fixture which makes it possible for the electricity to become a light. This is what is meant by the *as.* When we pray in faith we receive *what things soever* we pray for. If we believe that we shall receive them we shall receive *them.*

There is a specific, definite thing we are to receive, but we are to receive it *as* we believe. Let us say that we are praying for supply. Because we are praying for supply we are to receive supply, according to the principle that what things soever we believe when we pray, we shall receive. If we are praying for supply we shall receive supply, but the supply will be measured *as* we believe. The quantity of the supply must take the mold of our mental equivalent of supply.

Since we know that this, like all other principles, must be subject to definite law, and since we now understand the Law, let us again inquire into the consciousness that heals. It is recognition of the Principle, faith in the Principle, conviction that It will always respond, plus the knowledge that It can respond only by corresponding to our mental attitudes. This is the secret of the consciousness that heals.

Someone might ask whether we have left God, the warm, pulsating Divine Presence, out of this discussion. The answer is: "Certainly not." It is impossible to leave God out of anything, for do we not realize that God means the very

THE CONSCIOUSNESS THAT HEALS

Intelligence by which we understand this Law; the very consciousness by which we use It? Never forget that this Law, being the Law of Cause and Effect, is merely a mechanical force in the Universe, though an intelligent one. When it comes to the Law of Mind we must think of It this way, for this is the way to work. God is not left out. The very inspiration which causes us to inquire into this Law is the ever-present Spirit of God forever seeking Self-Expression through us. Unless our use of this Law is impulsed by Love and Unity we shall be automatically shut out from the most effective use of It.

Let us once more remind ourselves that the Universe is foolproof and that the Holy of Holies is entered only through the sanctuary of the heart, purified by Love, directed by Reason. The more feeling we put into our conviction, and the more faith we have in Divine Givingness, the more perfectly we shall be complying with the Law; hence we shall have greater power over It.

We should return, then, to our central theme with renewed hope and increased vigor, and most certainly with exuberant enthusiasm; with something of the spirit of an adventurer or explorer who goes out to discover new countries. The untold Good which the Creative Spirit has placed at our disposal waits the magic touch of our consciousness to spring into expression for us, filling the cup of our desire with Its manifold gifts. Who does not wish to be well, happy, and prosperous? Is there any normal person who desires to be inactive, impoverished, and in pain? Of course not! And is there not a voice within each of us forever proclaiming and insisting upon this Divine potentiality? This urge to express is natural.

Feeling unexpressed is frustration, but energy converted into action is accomplishment, and we can be certain that the Eternal is with us and never against us when we are never against any one else. Moreover, we can be certain that the prayer of faith will save the sick and God will raise him up. Let each, then, in his own way, lift up the chalice of his expectancy for the outpouring of the Spirit, that he may receive from It all that his soul can contain.

WHAT IS RELIGION?

Religion means our attitude toward God. This attitude is based on our concept of the relationship which exists between God the Universal Spirit, and man the individual spirit. If we believe that God is some far-off Divine Being from whom we are isolated, we shall give up in despair or our entire endeavor will be in seeking a reconciliation and reunion with this Divine Being.

We are compelled to think of the Spirit as either apart from us or within us, and if God is apart from us rather than a part of us, our search will be to reunite ourselves with this Divine Source of our being. Moreover, in our search we shall be laboring under the difficulty imposed by not knowing where to go or how to get there. But if we can conceive of the Divine Being as already existing within us, no search is necessary. Instead of a search there is an unfoldment.

Again, if we conceive of the Divine Being as separated from us, any communication must be across the void which separates us. From this viewpoint prayers, petitions, or attempts at communication with the Infinite must bridge some gap, cross some chasm, travel in some unknown direction with no certainty that they will reach their goal. Communion with the Infinite is possible only on the supposition that the Infinite is Omnipresent and, if Omnipresent, at the center of our own being.

All religions are attempts to interpret man's relationship with this indwelling and overarching Infinite, with a Spirit which fills all nature, all time, and all space with Its Presence. The purer the religion the more completely has it approached an attitude of Unity, a complete Oneness between God and man. Jesus boldly declared, *He that hath seen me hath seen the Father*. The purer the form of the religion the more perfectly has it presented the idea of an indwelling Presence which directly responds to man's thoughts.

The recognition that the Spirit thinks through our thought and expresses Itself through our act must necessarily create an intimacy which makes Divine communion more real and more beneficial than would any concept based on the thought of God as separate from our lives.

WHAT IS RELIGION?

A true religious concept is an indispensable aid in spiritual mind healing. The mental practitioner has a better chance of success when he believes in the indwelling Spirit, when he believes that God's work is already accomplished and perfect even though it is eternally unfolding. Moreover, his words will have more power when he believes that they are power, and he endows them with power in such degree as he senses the Divine Presence back of them.

This inner testimony of the soul is real and valid. Who could deny the artist the privilege of appreciating beauty? We all know that as a result of his sense of beauty he creates the beautiful, which is the object of art. We know that some artistic productions surpass others, and we recognize that back of them is a deep impression, a subjective feeling. We have not weighed or measured the reality which the artist contemplates, and yet we have evidence of it in his work.

The mental science practitioner whose mind is filled with spiritual awareness will speak a more powerful word than the one who rests his claim solely on the Law of Cause and Effect. The practitioner whose thought reaches the highest spiritual level will demonstrate that his word has the greatest power. The fact that the Law of Mind knows only how to obey and has no purpose of Its own to execute, demonstrates the proposition that a higher altitude of thought will find a corresponding higher level of manifestation, just as water will reach its own level by its own weight. It is in this sense that a true religious perspective is necessary to effective mental practice.

The Law, being a Doer and not a Knower, never acts of Itself; It merely reacts. The Word of Spirit is the enforcement of this Law. How can we expect a result to rise higher than its cause? It is self-evident that there is a coordinating Spirit and, as you will find continuously reaffirmed in these lessons, this coordinating Spirit must have within Itself a prototype or a perfect idea of every form.

A deep underlying sense of this Spiritual Universe is necessary to the most effective form of mind healing. To the technical work of the mental practitioner there should be added this deep spiritual sense of things. A subtle emanation of Spirit should flow through all the statements which he makes, for every statement must be based on the proposition of One God, One Man, and One Universe — a spiritual system which is complete, Divinely organized, spiritual not only in its origin but also in its manifestation.

WHAT IS RELIGION?

The spiritual mind healer must learn to see God in his patient. His conviction of this indwelling Divinity must be more than intellectual. For there is a field of Reality higher than the intellect, and it uses the intellect as its instrument. We should not decry the intellect since it gives shape and form to this inner feeling, but without the feeling nothing comes into being. This has been referred to as the Spirit and the letter of the Law, and we have been told that the letter without the Spirit does not quicken. Applied to mental healing this means that the words we speak must have a deep meaning to us, and we must sense that behind them there is a Power seeking expression.

This Power is infinitely greater than our intellect. The intellect does the best it can, but unless it is directed by the Spirit it finally succeeds in reaching only a gigantic negation, a complete denial of its own existence, a repudiation of the supreme fact of existence which is the act of directly experiencing Spirit.

You could not convince one who has had such an experience that it was an illusion or an hallucination, for this inner testimony of the soul is valid to the one who has it. It is just as much a part of him as is his thought, and the proof of its reality is evidenced by the results which it has produced in the lives of those who have been most deeply sensitive to love, truth, and beauty. To come into closer daily contact with this Supreme Source of wisdom and illumination should be the earnest desire of every worker in this field.

Appreciation of human experience will be quickened rather than retarded through unity with this indwelling Spirit. When a person learns to see God in everyone he will become more spontaneous. He will feel a deep and abiding inner joy.

Our spiritual experiences reach higher levels at some times than at others, and we should seek to bring the inspiration of these moments of illumination into our everyday living. If the philosophy of Christianity were lived wars would cease, unhappiness would cease, economic problems would be solved, poverty would be wiped from the face of the earth, and man's inhumanity to man would be transmuted into a spirit of mutual helpfulness.

This would not mean the reducing of all persons to one common level. We are individuals in a cosmic Wholeness. Each is a unique representation of the one and only Mind and Spirit, and since this Mind and Spirit is Infinite, Its capacity to individualize must likewise be without limit. Each may remain himself while seeing God in the other.

The spiritual mind practitioner should always have a sense of this fundamental Unity and should realize that it is continuously differentiating Itself through each one of us. Every man becomes a unique manifestation of the Whole, a microcosm within the Macrocosm; rooted in the Infinite, he personifies It. Some part of It, inseparable from It, remaining in It, he is still an individual. The paradox of the many and the One is explained not on the basis of a God apart from man, but on the basis of a God incarnated in man.

The religion of the spiritual mind healer must be one of Unity and Law. He must feel that he is one with the Spirit. Being one with this Self-Existent Spirit, he must sense that he uses the Law. There is nothing arrogant about this, for he knows that should such use be exercised in behalf of duality he himself must experience the effect of that very dualism which he attempts to project. The Universe is foolproof, and the profane do not enter the Holy of Holies.

Humility, reverence, and adoration are not to be confused with self-obliteration. We are not called upon to consider ourselves unholy; we are neither conceived in sin nor shapen in iniquity. Man's place in the creative order is as a dispenser of the Divine gifts, a husbandman of the indwelling Lord.

The morbidity which has come with the sense of isolation and separation from God must be healed if joy and laughter are to take the place of sorrow and tears. How can we believe in a weeping Universe or a sad God or a melancholy First Cause? Such concepts would contradict the fundamental necessity of Reality, that God is a synonym for Wholeness.

Negation does not belong to the Infinite, and being undivided It is never separated from Its own Good. We must arrive at an abiding sense of our Unity with Good. Much that we have believed must be discarded, for we can never avoid the conclusion that with what judgment we have judged, by that same judgment we must ourselves be judged.

The approach to Reality should be simple, direct, and spontaneous. The Secret

Place of the Most High is neither in the holy mountain of Samaria nor at Jerusalem; *for, behold, the Kingdom of God is within you.* This Kingdom is finished, complete, and perfect for eternity, but the manifestation of this Kingdom is the eternal activity of right ideas, law, order, truth, and beauty. Man is given dominion in this Kingdom by a fundamental necessity of his nature. It is impossible that this dominion should be withheld from him.

There is no deific power which either withdraws from man or advances toward man. No more of God is in one place than in another, and in the place where man is, God is, and where man recognizes the Divine Presence, there the Divine Presence responds — not some of It, but all of It.

The communion of the soul with this Over-Presence is a natural act. To feel that a Presence greater than we are is guiding us is normal. To trust this Presence is sanity. To desire that the Divine Eternal shall project Itself through our thought is to be receptive to that greater side of our nature which lies open to the upper reaches of thought. This is religion.

BIBLES OF THE WORLD

Fragments from the spiritual history of the race revealing the fundamental Unity of religious thought and experience.

JUDAISM and CHRISTIANITY

But to us there is but One God, the Father, of whom are all things, and we in Him.

And thou shalt love the Lord thy God with all thy heart, and with all thy soul, and with all thy might.

HINDUISM

He is the Creator, He the Disposer. He Himself is one, single, one only.

How many gods are there?

One! I know that Person, the Last Source of every soul.

ISLAM

Your God is One God.

He is the Lord of the East. He is the Lord of the West.

SIKHISM

The True One was in the beginning.

The True One is now. The True One also shall be.

TAOISM

There is a Being wondrous and complete. Before heaven and earth It was. How calm It is! How Spiritual!

Alone It standeth; and It changeth not. Around It moveth; and It suffereth not. Yet therefore can It be called the World's Mother.

SHINTOISM

When the sky is clear, and the wind hums in the fir-trees; 'tis the heart of God Who thus reveals Himself.

CONFUCIANISM

Heaven will give great blessing.

MEDITATION

I know there is but One Power in the Universe, and this Power is God. This Power manifests in and through all form, all people, all conditions, and is at the very center of my being.

This God-Power I AM

This Power is Life Itself, and Its nature is Love. It contains all Wisdom, Peace, Strength. At the center of my being I feel this Perfection in me. I know It is all around me. Everywhere I turn I behold It. It is my whole being. Every cell and atom of my being, my every thought and feeling, my every act is an expression of this God-Power.

The Intelligence within me is constantly guiding me. Clearly I see the right thing for me to do; I know the right thing for me to say in every circumstance. This God-Intelligence within me deals with every situation harmoniously. I find life thrilling, stimulating.

I know that Love protects Its own. I know that Love now makes clear the way before me, eliminating every seeming obstruction. I am guided into an ever-widening unfoldment of being, and I rest in perfect peace.

One with all Life, my every need is now fulfilled.

LESSON 7

SUBJECTIVE CREATIVE MEDIUM

The Law of Mind in Action

A Message from Ernest Holmes

Perhaps by this time you are wondering why we put so much stress on the Law of Mind in Action, and why we so often repeat the same thoughts. The answer is that this whole series of lessons deals with but a few fundamental principles which must be stated over and over again in order that they may be kept at the point of your attention. There is no other way to teach a science.

Every science has a fundamental principle governing it. Our basic Principle is Universal Mind, the use of which we call the Law of Mind in Action. We set this Mind Principle in motion through our thinking, whether or not we know it. The Law and the Word are what we deal with, and our word becomes the law of our experience.

Our word uses the Law, and we are not responsible for Its action any more than an electrician is responsible for the action of electric energy in ringing a doorbell. He uses a law for his purposes and the law responds. The Law is a doer but not a knower. The electrician is the knower.

So in using the Law of Mind in Action you are the knower, the Law is the Doer. You are not responsible for the operation of the Law, but you are responsible for the way you use It. Therefore be certain that you use It definitely and consistently, and in such a way that you will be glad to experience Its action.

SUBJECTIVE CREATIVE MEDIUM
The Law of Mind in Action

(textbook reference: pages 92-97)

This lesson further explains that the creative medium of Spirit, which is the Universal Soul or Subjective Mind, is the mental Law of the Universe. A law that is subjective must of necessity be subject to the intelligence which uses it. Page 403 explains that *the Law of Mind is not selective.*

Of Itself the Law has nothing to say about the ideas that are put into It. It knows how to create them into form and must do so mathematically, but It has no selectivity. Like electricity, which has no conscious knowledge as to whether it is to become light or heat, the Law of Mind has no self-conscious determination. The self-conscious determination is in the Spirit which uses the Law, and man is Spirit.

It is this understanding that will enable you to use the Law for other people. When you say to yourself, "This word which I am now speaking is for John Smith, who lives at 108 West Seventh Street, New York City," you are conscious that you are using the Law for this particular John Smith who lives at this specific address, and you are conscious that the Law is operating on your thought for him. It has no selectivity of Itself — you are choosing what It shall do. You are the knower; the Law is the Doer. It knows how to create without knowing why It is creating and without having any choice whatsoever.

The first three paragraphs on page 347 explain further the meaning of Subjective Mind. Particularly seek a clear realization of the meaning of the words in *italics.* For it is only when we see that what we call *our* subjective mind is merely our individual use of the Creative Law of the Universe, that we shall be able to have a real scientific approach to the subject, and only when we have a scientific approach can we expect to make conscious and definite use of the Creative Law.

SUBJECTIVE CREATIVE MEDIUM

As a practitioner you must always know what you are doing and why you are doing it, as well as how to do it. As a result of the word you have spoken you must have implicit confidence that your decree in the Law will produce a definite physical manifestation in whatever direction you turn your attention.

Law is defined as *Mind in Action* (page 605). Study the entire definition. While there is no limit to the Law, there appears to be a limit to man's use of It. This means that even though the Law of Creativity is Infinite, we shall draw from It only as much Good as our measure will hold, no more, no less. This brings us back to the central theme of our entire course of study — the Universal Creative Spirit of God creates by Self-Knowing or Contemplation. Man, being the image and likeness of the Universal Creative Spirit, must act in accordance with his nature; that is, he creates by contemplation or self-knowing. This is the explanation of the great saying of Jesus: *And ye shall know the truth, and the truth shall make you free.*

It is evident that if the knowing of something can produce freedom there must be a law which automatically reacts to our knowing. It is of utmost importance that the Laws of Mind and Spirit be understood. When you treat for a physical or a financial betterment in some other person's experience you must be conscious that his good is now made manifest, and in such degree as you are aware of that good it will appear in his experience.

Becoming aware of his good is an interior awareness. It is something the mind does to itself, and as a result of this self-recognition, self-knowingness, or state of consciousness as it is often called, the Law which automatically reacts to this self-knowingness produces an objective form, a physical condition which exactly balances and equals the self-knowingness, just as water reaches its own level by its own weight.

Spirit and Law were never created. They coexist; they are a part of the Eternal Reality. The Law which man uses, the Mind which he uses, and the Spirit which he is, are all One. Again let us consider the fact that there is no such thing as *your* mind, *my* mind, *his* mind, *her* mind. Mind is an Eternal Principle in the Universe, and when we think, we are making use of It, and as we think, we are individualizing It. This individualization of It we speak of as *myself.*

Just as all physical nature is made up of One Ultimate Stuff, which includes our physical bodies, and just as each body is a peculiar individualization of that Stuff, so all individual mentalities emerge from one Universal Mind. We should think of ourselves as being in such complete unity with this Mind that there are no longer two — only One. As we think inside our own being, we think upon the Only Being.

The next great step which the psychologist will be compelled to take will be the recognition of the Unity of Mind. But this Unity of Mind will never contradict a diversity of thought; hence there is no real restriction in this idea; indeed it is the only guarantee we could have of a complete freedom.

If you will carefully study the fourth and fifth paragraphs on page 93 you will realize the significance of the idea that every time we think we are using this Universal Creative Medium. In the first paragraph on page 406, Spirit is referred to as being present in Its entirety at all times. It follows that all of Spirit is wherever we center our thought. Therefore the Truth in Its entirety is ever with us, ever available. Spiritual inspiration always awaits our recognition, and Divine guidance waits on our consent. The Spirit flows through us as an outlet for Its own Self-Expression.

Mind is in the realm of causes. Conditions are in the realm of effects . . . New thoughts create new conditions (page 406, last paragraph). The new condition will be created in such degree as the subjective state of our thought becomes clarified. The subjective state of our thought becomes clarified as we consciously determine to think only of what we wish to have happen.

This is not always easy, but we must realize that the Law of God is one of liberty (read page 488). Freedom already exists, like truth and beauty, but it exists in an abstract and formless state. It can only take the form which thought gives it; therefore you will see that the thought of limitation creates the very limitation conceived by that thought. Freedom and bondage are merely two ways of expressing a limitless possibility.

If we wish freedom we must be conscious of freedom, and since the idea of God as a symbol of spiritual liberty gives us the greatest concept of freedom, it follows that the more completely we spiritualize our thought the freer we shall become. To dwell upon lack is to create it; to think of disease is to perpetuate it;

to remain unhappy is to attract unhappy situations. There is no other way to objectify that which we desire than to turn deliberately and definitely from that which hurts.

But we all, with open face beholding as in a glass the glory of the Lord, are changed into the same image from glory to glory, even as by the Spirit of the Lord (page 489). There is already a spiritual realm within the mind which knows these things; hence we must turn to this Great Within and with uplifted thought become receptive to this Divine Influx. This is the meaning of the paragraph at the top of page 480. It is really the unfoldment of Spirit through our own consciousness and in our own act.

At the top of page 94 we find that we cannot expect one thought to be creative while another kind of thought remains unproductive. We may as well set it down as a law that all thought must be creative, but since the Universe is not a duality but a Unity, thoughts of Good destroy thoughts of evil just as the light overcomes the darkness. It does this without argument and without contention. As this paragraph states, when we declare the Truth about anyone, the speaking of his name directs the Law for him in a specific and definite way, in an individual and personal way.

It is not always easy to see that this mental work is done at the center of our own being; that is, that the practitioner treats himself in order to help his patient. But we are sure that by now you will understand how this Principle operates. Man's consciousness is a point in the Infinite. Therefore man's consciousness is the Infinite, not limited, but taking the form of his thought.

It does not limit the Infinite to take a particular form any more than we could say that a flea has less life than an elephant because it is smaller. Life in Its entirety and in Its intensity exists at any and every point, and each man is a point in the consciousness of the Universe. Hence when he thinks within himself he thinks upon It, and when he directs his thought within himself he directs his thought within It. That is how his word becomes Law.

If you will read the paragraph under *Mind and Ether,* page 94, you will see that the laws of attraction and repulsion, gravitation, adhesion and cohesion, etc. (which from the standpoint of physical science operate through the ethers or upon the ethers), must be exact physical correspondents of the more subtle mental law which says that thought operates upon Mind. From this viewpoint — and we believe it to be a true one — attraction and repulsion, adhesion and cohesion, are primarily mental concepts. This we know to be true, that the law of attraction is a mental thing.

Turn to page 534, to the Meditation called *My Atmosphere.* In reading these words carefully and thoughtfully, over and over again, let them stimulate your imagination to an active belief that you are a Divine Center of Spiritual Causation. As the consciousness or realization of your own true being dawns in your thought, realize that you have arrived at a place of Spiritual Power.

The next step is to use this Power for a definite purpose, to treat specifically for yourself or someone else. Sense the Power back of your words but do not try to put any power into them. We need conviction, not power — Power already is, while conviction may be lacking. Do not practice any method of concentration or the holding of thoughts; merely be still, but definitely know in the silence of your own soul that some desired Good is taking place. In this way you are certain to demonstrate.

On page 499, under the heading, *Doers of the Word,* we find: *What we know we can do.* We are told to be doers of the word, and not hearers only. As our spiritual comprehension increases we should be able to make better and better demonstrations, both for ourselves and for others. This will call for a calm, persistent, insistent determination to believe and to mentally act on that belief. Whatever stimulates our faith, whatever inspires us, will be an aid in this demonstration.

What is it that we wish to demonstrate? We wish to demonstrate that spiritual thought forms, or spiritual consciousness, actually overcome physical conditions; that each one of us has the power to control his destiny, to help and to heal others, and that there is a place at the center of every man's being where the Infinite and Almighty is eternally enthroned. *The Will of God is always toward that which expresses life and happiness* (page 412, third paragraph).

We need not be afraid of using our Divine Power, nor need we fear that we are usurping the throne of God. This *is* the throne of God. Please read paragraphs 2, 3, and 4, page 404, which will explain to you the result of fear — how it blocks the givingness of the Spirit, how it produces a sense of limitation because it is a denial of the Divine Givingness. God never withholds any Good from His creation. And as we more completely realize this we shall change bondage for freedom and sadness for happiness.

You will find a very helpful suggestion for the practice of this Divine Consciousness on page 358, second paragraph, where it speaks of providing the mental equivalents of life; creating a spiritual consciousness in our own thought which is equivalent to our desires. It is both reasonable and rational to desire the good, the beautiful, and the true.

There is nothing wrong in our desire to be free from pain and lack, sickness, want, and limitation, any more than there is anything wrong in desiring the end of war or pestilence, famine, or poverty in the world. As a matter of fact the more completely the righteous prove that God is all there is, the sooner wars and human contention will cease. *For all they that take the sword shall perish with the sword.*

On page 95 the question is asked, *How can Spirit create?* Well, we shall never be able to answer this question. That is the miracle of Life Itself. Remember, the Truth is that which is — birthless, deathless, and changeless. How are you going to explain your own life? By experience and through faith we accept life and the laws of nature. So accept your own Divinity, accept the Power that is within you, but use this Power definitely and for specific purposes.

At the bottom of page 95 we are told that we must be careful not to divide Mind against Itself when we speak of the subjective, the subconscious, and the conscious. There will be no danger here if you are always careful to realize that the Spirit is the Conscious Mind, and that which we call the subconscious mind is merely the Law of Mind in Action.

From this viewpoint (see page 97) the subjective mind is never an entity. *Each person in his objective state is a distinct and individualized center in Universal Mind, but in his* subjective *state . . . each is Universal* (page 352).

SUMMARY

The Law of Mind is not selective; It is reactive only. The creative soil in your garden does not care whether you are planting tomatoes or cucumbers. When you say tomatoes it answers by producing tomatoes, as though it also said tomatoes, and when you say cucumbers it responds by saying cucumbers or producing cucumbers. It has no self-determination. All laws are like this, and the Law of Mind is no exception to the general rule. Therefore as a practitioner you must know what you are doing and why.

There is no limit to the Law Itself. Any limitation is in the way we use It. Neither the Spirit nor the Law was ever created. They are coexistent and coeternal. They are a part of what is.

Since the Spirit is One and Undivided, all of It is wherever we center our thought. We do not go anywhere to find It. It is right where we are. Freedom already exists. Freedom and bondage are the same thing in that they are but two ways of using One Principle. Abundance, success, and happiness are in our own thinking.

We sense the Power back of our word but make no attempt to put any Power into it. Conviction, faith, and acceptance give Power to our word. The way we use the Law decides what It is going to do for us.

Each one individualizes the Universal Spirit. We are what the ancients called a microcosm within a Macrocosm — a little world within a Big World.

The Creative Power which is at the center of everything is discovered in our own consciousness.

QUESTIONS

Brief answers to these questions should be written out by the student after studying this lesson, and the answers compared with those in the Appendix.

1. What is meant by the creative medium of Spirit?

2. In speaking of the Creative Law of Mind, what do we mean by *intelligent but subjective*?

3. Why is it that you can direct the mental law for others?

4. What is our subjective mind?

5. How should a practitioner feel about his word?

6. What is meant by the Self-Contemplation of Spirit?

7. Do the Self-Contemplation and Self-Knowingness of Spirit have the same meaning as the Word of God?

8. What is the next great step that psychology must take?

9. When do we use the Creative Principle?

10. Why is it that new thoughts create new conditions?

11. How do we change our thought patterns in order to create more desirable conditions?

12. Are negative thoughts such as bondage, poverty, fear, sickness, etc., equal in creative power to the positive thoughts of freedom, abundance, faith, wholeness, etc.?

13. What do we mean by declaring the Truth about someone?

14. Where does spiritual or mental treatment take place?

15. How can a treatment which is given in the thought of the practitioner affect his patient?

16. What place have power and conviction in mental treatment?

17. In the Science of Mind what do we seek to demonstrate?

18. Can we explain the Creative Power within us?

19. Is our philosophy weak because we cannot explain the Creative Power within us?

20. Do we divide Mind against Itself when we speak of the conscious, subconscious, subjective, etc.?

METAPHYSICAL INTERPRETATIONS OF THE BIBLE

based on

Thomas Troward's *Bible Mystery and Bible Meaning*

THE NAME OF THE UNKNOWN

In his chapter *The Sacred Name,* Troward informs us that according to ancient tradition, *the knowledge of the secret Name of God enables him who possesses it to perform the most stupendous miracles.* He suggests that it is the office of the name of anything to convey to us the idea of its whole nature; accordingly the correct Name of God should be a concise statement of the Divine Nature as the Source of all Life, Wisdom, and Goodness, and the Origin of all manifested being.

The Secret Name, therefore, suggests the nature of Reality Itself. The realization of this Reality opens up the wellsprings of our Being and enables us to drink from that perennial fountain of life which Jesus referred to when he said that if one drinks from this fount he shall never thirst again.

Troward makes plain that while the Bible refers to Reality under a variety of terms and names, each of them has practically the same meaning, *since each suggests some particular aspect of THAT which is the all-embracing UNITY.* This is also true of other sacred literature. *Realize that thou art "That" Brahma, which is the cessation of all differentiation . . . eternally unconditioned and undivided.* What is this but a statement of the Nameless One? *The Tao, considered as unchanging, has no name;* and from Hermes: *Immovable God alone, and rightly alone; for He Himself is in Himself, and by Himself, and round Himself. . . .* This means that the Infinite Creative Cause, being all that is, makes things out of Itself by Itself becoming the thing which It makes.

In Job we find this statement: *Canst thou by searching find out God? canst thou find out the Almighty unto perfection?* God is not found in the stone and yet God is the stone. By searching outwardly we do not discover the Nameless One, but when we stop searching, become still and know, the Name of the Nameless proclaims Itself through us. The Upanishads say, *Not in the sight abides his form, none beholds him by the eye. Those who know him dwelling in the heart and mind become immortal.* From the Gita: *But verily thou art not able to behold Me with these thine eyes; the divine eye I give unto thee.* This has also been referred to in mythology as the All-seeing Eye. One instantly recognizes that all these presentations refer to That Something in the Universe which is Absolute Cause, That which, being Formless, gives birth to form; Timeless, It projects all time; without Itself moving, everything moves within It. It is the One Unity within which all differentiation takes place.

Troward tells us that the name Jehovah signifies *Unity passing into manifestation as the Multiplicity of all individual beings.* This Unity includes both the active and passive factors; both the masculine and the feminine natures, the Father Principle and the Mother Principle. The Father Principle represents Absolute Being, but since Absolute Being must have an object of Its being, that is, since cause must be cause to something in order to exist as cause, the Creative Cause must have a Son. Or, as Hippolytus stated, *For He* [God] *was . . . all love; but love is not love unless there be an object of love.* This means that the Divine Creative Cause must become Father to something in order that It may experience Its own Being. And that to which It gives birth must be born out of law and order; hence the Divine Mother Principle so often referred to in antiquity, particularly in ancient Hindu symbols. For as the Divine Father Principle represents the impregnating Principle of Self-assertion, so the Divine Mother Principle represents the feminine or receptive aspect of the manifesting Spirit which brings forth the forms of creation. thus in one of the ancient writings we find this: *Like a mother to her subjects, intent on their welfare . . . She* [referring to the Mother Principle] *was the most eminent of Goddesses to the whole world.*

Implied in the Sacred Name we have a combination of that which projects and that which gives form. Not as though they were two principles in nature but two aspects of One Principle: a dual unity. It is the union of this masculine and feminine which gives birth to all form. In our terminology we say that thought operating through the creative field of Mind produces condition. From this standpoint the conscious projection of thought represents the Creative Principle in Its masculine aspect, while the Law of Mind represents the Creative Principle in Its feminine or productive aspect. It is the union of the Word with the Law which gives birth to creation.

The Nameless One is that Reality which ancient scriptures refer to as something which was not born and cannot die. *There is no beginning or end to the Tao. There is but one Brahma which is Truth's Self, it is from ignorance of that one that Godheads have been conceived as diverse. . . .* (Mahabharata). This means that Reality is One, but being confused over multiplicity we have given many names to this One. These names are diverse and they largely contradict each other. We do not understand that Cause and Effect are but two ends of the same thing. We are confused when we view only the effect.

We are of a like nature with Reality Itself, but since we have become confused by looking upon the multiplicity of effects which rise in One Reality, we have come to believe in a multiplicity of causes. The Upanishads say, . . . *so over rules the All Glorious, Adorable God; One alone, all that exists is likeness with its cause.* And from Hermes: *The Oneness, being Source and Root of all, is in all things as Root and Source. Without [this] Source is naught; whereas the Source [Itself] is from naught but Itself.* The Gita tells us: *When he (anyone) perceiveth a diversified existence of beings as rooted in One, and spreading forth from It, then he reacheth the eternal.* In Revelation we read: *I am Alpha and Omega, the beginning and the end. . . .* And in the Psalms we have a poetical description of this Unity of all life: *Whither shall I go from thy spirit? or whither shall I flee from thy presence? If I ascend up into heaven, thou art there . . . If I take the wings of the morning, and dwell in the uttermost parts of the sea; Even there shall thy hand lead me. . . .*

The Sacred Name contains everything that is implied in the meaning of cause, medium, and effect; God, man, and creation. It implies a complete and absolute unity of all life. Troward sums up his findings by stating that the name Jehovah contains in Itself the Three Fundamental Principles of the Universe — the Unity, the Duality, and the Trinity, and by their inclusion in a single word affirms that there is no contradiction between them, but that they are all necessary phases of the Universal Truth which is only ONE.

Next Troward takes up a study of the Lost Word, which Word is a symbol of the Life Principle as It expresses on each and all planes. In the Egyptian Book of the Dead we find this statement: *I concur by this most mighty word . . . and "I Am" brings to my remembrance in Him what I had forgotten.* This is a definite reference to the Word of Power which is a symbol of the higher qualities and of wisdom. Troward tells us that the Lost Word, or Word of Power, is also the Sacred

Name, and he refers us to Deuteronomy 30:14 where it says, *But the word is very nigh unto thee, in thy mouth, and in thy heart. . . .* The Sacred Name is *I AM.* Troward tells us that this is the Divine Name revealed to Moses at the burning bush and is the Word enshrined in the name Jehovah. Thus he said, *The Word of Power is close at hand to every one, and it continues to be the Lost Word only because of our ignorance. . . .*

Jesus prayed, *Our Father which art in heaven, Hallowed be thy name.* Since he had located the Kingdom of Heaven within, was he not then addressing the Divine Being at the center of his and of every man's soul? And the Text of Taoism states: *The Tao does not exhaust Itself in what is greatest, nor is It ever absent from what is least; and therefore it is to be found complete and diffused in all things.* In the Gita it says, *I, the Father of this universe, the Mother, the Supporter, the Grandsire, the Holy One to be known, the Word of Power.* This refers to the *Father which art in heaven,* in everything. And the Father, and Heaven, man, his world, creation, all are One. Or as we find in I John 5:7: *For there are three that bear record in heaven, the Father, the Word, and the Holy Ghost: and these three are one.*

The word of power is *I AM,* signifying the essence of being. In the Egyptian Book of the Dead we read: *For "I Am" is my rest in His seasons.* The *I AM* is the true individuality and has been called The First Born. The *I AM,* as we have already discussed, is Universal as God and individual as man. Again from the Egyptian Book of the Dead: *For "I Am" is that God even . . . the Lord of hosts. . . .* In Yogi philosophy we read: *The ego is beyond all disease, not within the reach of comprehension, free from all imagination, and all pervading.* Also a quotation from the Apocrypha: *And I appointed him as ruler on earth, to have wisdom and there was no one like him. . . .* In Hebrews: *Thou madest him a little lower than the angels; thou crownest him with glory and honour. . . Thou hast put all things in subjection under his feet.* And from Hermes: *The soul however, is not forever in a mortal body, for it can be without a body.* Jesus referred to the *I AM* as the Way, the Truth, and the Life. He also said, *I am the resurrection and the life.*

Resurrection means passing from a lower to a higher place, from a lesser to a greater comprehension of life. *I am the resurrection* refers to the God Principle in us that Jesus talked so much about. The Power and Intelligence through which we expand our consciousness is this Living Spirit within. God the Eternal

THE NAME OF THE UNKNOWN

I AM is in everything; God the individualized *I* is at the very center of our being.

Unless we believe in and embody the Spiritual Principle within us we shall continue in our mistakes. The purifying principle of experience, suffering, etc., which purges us from our mistakes, has been likened to Purgatory, Hades, the Regions of Darkness. It has also been likened to Sheol, a place for the burning of garbage. It is generally considered that all such figures of speech are symbolic of the lower planes which have been called mental, astral, etheric, and physical. These planes become purged in the all-consuming fire of Spirit which burns out the dross of human experience, leaving nothing but the incarnation of the Eternal *I AM*, the Ego.

Troward tells us that the true recognition of the *I AM* is the recognition of the Self. This true Self is always one with the Infinite. Next he refers to the Mystical Marriage, the union of the soul with its Source. This refers to the conscious union of the Word of Spirit with the creative Principle of Mind. In Meade's comments on Hermes we read: *But the chief of all mysteries for Philo was apparently the Sacred Marriage, the mystic union of the soul as female, with God as male.* The Mystical Marriage like the New Birth is something which is forever taking place. The resurrection from the lower to the higher, or the lesser to the greater, is a process of eternal evolution or expansion. What is this other than a discovery that, as Troward says, the whole principle of being is in ourselves?

It is evident that until we understand our relationship with the Eternal we continue to perish in our mistakes. That is, we continue to transgress the Law of rightness or righteousness. Since ignorance of the Law excuses no one from Its consequences, we suffer until the lesson is learned. It does not necessarily follow that this is because of viciousness, but largely because of ignorance.

One of the most interesting illustrations Troward draws is that the Bible is the picture book of the evolution of man. In referring to the burning bush he tells us that *bush* represents wood or matter or the material universe, and *burning* represents Spirit. Hence the burning bush signifies the union of Spirit and matter into a single whole. The bush is not consumed, but burns with a Celestial Light, with the Light Eternal which is in and through everything. Thus all creation proclaims the luminous *I AM*.

THE NAME OF THE UNKNOWN

Troward next explains that just as there is a Sacred Name for all nature, there is a Sacred Name for man, and we all remember that it is written that there is no other Name whereby we can become saved. Here again we must realize that salvation is not from a power of darkness but rather from the darkness of ignorance.

The name Jesus was commonly used, as it is today in most Latin countries. Jesus represents the son of man; Christ represents the hidden or true Man whose kingdom is not of this world. Jesus, the son of man, the son of a lowly carpenter, becomes Christ, the Son of God. Isaiah refers to this when he speaks of the son of the virgin as named Emmanuel, which means God-with-us. The blood that flows from Emmanuel's veins is symbolic of the life-giving energy of Spirit pouring Itself from the Christ Principle, which is the Son of God, into the Jesus Principle, which is the son of man. This is why we are told: *And whatsoever ye do in word or deed, do all in the name of the Lord Jesus, giving thanks to God and the Father by him.*

This reference to the name of the Lord Jesus is not merely to an historic character, howsoever benign; it also refers to the indwelling Principle which Jesus located at the center of every man's being. In this way the name of God becomes the name of man, since it is Emmanuel or God-with-us, God immanent in us. It is the discovery that *unto us a child is born.* This child is the Son of God referred to in the New Testament in this passage: *The Spirit itself beareth witness with our spirit that we are the children of God.*

The birth of Christ is symbolic of the higher nature impregnating the human soul. It is as Campbell suggests, . . . *the discovery and exercise of our highest faculties,* sometimes referred to in the East as the Atma-buddhi energizing on the higher plane. The First Adam is of the earth, earthy, and liable to death; the Second is from Heaven and triumphant over death. In Luke 21:27-28 we read: *And then shall they see the Son of man coming in a cloud with power and great glory . . . then look up, and lift up your heads; for your redemption draweth nigh.* This is symbolic of the incarnation consciously recognized as the living essence of one's own being. This deific birth into the soul, coming from the clouds, means the descent of Spirit into the lower mind.

Phillips Brooks said, *It may be that the clouds that for us mortals haunt that land of righteousness and truth, may long hang so thick and low that living close to Him the soul may still fail to see Him, but some day certainly the fog shall rise, and the clouds shall scatter, and in perfect enlightenment of the other life, the soul shall see its Lord. . . .* Lord is symbolic of the higher self. The Wonderful Child which appears when we look up through the clouds is the Eternal *I AM* reflecting and incarnating Itself in us. *And it is the Spirit that beareth witness, because the Spirit is truth* (John 5:6).

In the Egyptian Book of the Dead we find this remarkable concept: *"We will not let thee enter into us," say the bolts of this door, "Unless thou tellest our names."* And it goes on to reveal that the names are Right and Truth. We must look through the clouds of obscurity to Right, to Truth, to the very Source of Life Itself. *For with thee is the fountain of life: in thy light shall we see light* (Psalm 36:9). It is light that dissipates the clouds. It is Truth that dissipates error.

It is evident that as the name of God is *I AM,* so the name of the son or the child which is born into the consciousness of sonship is also *I AM.* Troward tells us the individual is illuminated through realizing that he himself is a personification of the Universal Spirit. Thus the Eternal *I AM* is at the root of our individualized being. The proverb of Solon, the Athenian lawgiver, *Know Thyself,* is an admonition to discover the nature of our own being and to realize that the name of the Father and the name of the son are One. It is from a recognition of the union of the Father with the son that knowledge is found and salvation gained.

In St. John 1:12 it is written: *But as many as received him, to them gave he power to become the sons of God, even to them that believe on his name.* When we recognize our union with Good and live in compliance with this recognition, Spiritual Power is automatically delivered to us. The Sacred Name must of necessity be the word of power, for it is nothing less than the original creative Spirit operating through our own minds.

It would be impossible to suppose a greater union than that which is inherent in the nature of our own being. The God-Principle within us constitutes the whole Reality of our being. Living in conformity with this Principle, in conjunction with Its Divine Will, we are automatically given as much power as we can conceive. But this power is never one of disunion, since the Principle of Reality can never be divided against Itself. Thus the Apostle James tells us that we ask and receive not because we ask amiss; we ask contrary to the Divine Nature, which is Love, Truth, Beauty, and Wisdom.

No doubt the entire search of humanity has been, consciously or unconsciously, a search for Divine Wisdom, for somehow or other we feel that there is a wisdom from which power must flow. This is an intuitive perception; thus it comes from the highest faculty in man, the true Atma, Christ, or High Counselor within us. We desire wisdom and power because there is an incessant urge toward self-expression within all. We wish more completely to enter into the joy of living. We wish certainty for uncertainty, faith for fear, life for death. This is not only natural but right, and a wisdom greater than our own impels this search toward Reality.

How wonderful it would be to discover the Sacred Name embosomed in our own being; that the Child who is called Wonderful is already in our soul; that salvation is from within through the recognition of the Divine at the center of our own being. To *be still and know that I am God* means to be alone in our own consciousness with the realization that all Power is delivered to the uses of Goodness.

As we meditate in the silence of our consciousness, thinking deeply upon the meaning of the Name hidden in the soul, shall not the New Birth take place through us as it does forever in all creation? Shall not the waste places of our lives, like the burning bush of old, leap into flames radiating a warmth and glow which bring wholeness and peace?

THE PRINCIPLE OF MIND AT WORK

Unless the one studying spiritual mind healing practices this Principle he will neither understand its nature nor appreciate its value. Therefore its practical application becomes of prime importance, and each of us should become a practitioner even if he himself is his only patient.

Like any other principle in nature, we must use this consciously and deliberately. The practitioner resolves things into thoughts, for it stands to reason that only thought can reach that which is the result of thought. We do not expect thought to reach some physical condition independent of mind. If there is such a thing as mental healing it must be based on the supposition that all form is a manifestation of mind and that mind controls its manifestation.

From the standpoint of the mental practitioner disease must be seen as primarily a thing of thought, and the diseased condition as a mental declaration of discord, an argument of confusion, or a mental experience of negation. It is the wrong kind of manifestation, and whether or not we believe that it originates in mind, the mental practitioner must confine his work to the operation of thought, for this is his field.

The mental practitioner resolves things into thoughts and proceeds to untangle the wrong thought through the recognition of the Omnipresence of God or Truth. Mind can never operate outside of consciousness, and if the practitioner believes that disease or conditions are external to consciousness, and treats them as if they were, he will soon discover that he is trying to bombard them from without. He is trying to make mind reach something which is not mental, or trying to make thought reach something which is outside of mind. He is doomed to failure.

When he realizes that everything is either Mind in an absolute state, or mind in a concrete form, he has no difficulty in rearranging thought positively instead of negatively. This is exactly what a spiritual mind practitioner does. He does this deliberately and consciously. The name of a disease signifies to him merely the thought about the disease, whether a person believes it to be curable or incurable, whether he believes it will take a long time or a short time to heal, and it signifies the mental reaction of the race consciousness. This is the only significance the name can have to the practitioner, for in this field he cannot treat one disease as organic and another disease as functional, since from the standpoint of our practice all disease is a negative statement in mind.

Now I am fully aware that the thought that all disease is a negative statement in mind is a rather difficult one to understand, and is likely to produce considerable confusion in the minds of those who hear it for the first time. But let us remember that this field is entirely different from other fields. Here we have a practitioner who treats through the instrument of thought alone. He is not antagonizing any other form or method of practice; he is not refusing his patient the right to have any other form of practice even while he is being treated mentally.

He is a spiritual mind practitioner, and from his viewpoint, no matter what the condition is and no matter what it has been pronounced to be, it must remain a thing of thought, for as already stated, if it is not thought, how is thought going to reach it? And the practitioner is thoroughly convinced that thought does reach it, that pure Mind exists everywhere, and that pure Mind is at the very center of the diseased condition.

The practitioner must conceive of pure Mind as being in a state of harmony. Instead of feeling that he is treating some terrible disease he feels that he is explaining why this negative condition need not be. His explanation is to himself about his patient; it is never to his patient. What, then, is he doing? He is clearing up his own consciousness, and in order to do this he must resolve the disease into a thing of thought.

The practitioner uses any statement about a particular case which will untie the mental knots in his own consciousness about his patient. Generally he is confronted with the idea of fear, and he should begin his treatment by removing all sense of fear. He must know that there is nothing of which to be afraid and he must make a definite statement not only that there is nothing of which to be afraid, but that there is no one to be afraid. He must say this for his patient, not *to* his patient but *about* him. When giving a treatment he never addresses the patient by name or speaks to him personally in mind; he merely identifies his treatment with his patient by saying, "This treatment is for so-and-so," and then he forgets all about his patient objectively and gives the treatment within his own consciousness.

If God is All in All there is nothing of which to be afraid, for perfect love casts out fear; where love is, fear cannot enter. The practitioner knows that fear cannot operate through his patient or through anyone around him. Man is a spiritual entity; therefore he has no disease, nothing which is opposed to life assails him, nothing is operating through him which can produce death, since there is no death.

If he is using the argumentative method of treating he brings an array of arguments to support his position that God is All in All, and to reject the belief that it is necessary for his patient to suffer from this particular disease, or any other. The form of the argument and the power of the argument is merely to produce realization. Argument itself is not realization any more than musical technique is harmony. The argument merely gives form, definite intention, specific direction to the treatment. Argument leads toward a realization of the Allness of Good. Probably more people are helped through argument than by any other method, although in every instance one should seek a growing conviction and an increasing realization of the meaning of one's argument.

The Life Principle Itself is the healer, or if one chooses to put it this way, God is the healer. The patient is a spiritual entity and there is nothing about a spiritual entity that needs to be healed. Disease of itself is not person, place, or thing, and has no location. It did not begin in time, it has no duration in time, it does not end anywhere in time. It is no longer being experienced in the consciousness of the one who has been affected by it. These are merely suggested arguments for the purpose of clearing up the mind of the practitioner, for his thought is the only thought that he can heal in this practice.

The practitioner assumes that the Body of God is perfect, including every manifestation of Itself. Man is the Body of God. For instance, the idea of vision, of speech, or of any other faculty or organ of the body is an Eternal Idea, an Infinite Idea, and an Omnipresent Idea.

The practitioner treats to know that there is only one Perfect Pattern of lung or heart; there is only one Idea of lung or heart, because there is only one Spirit, one Absolute *I AM,* one Eternal God, or one everlasting Reality. The heart God made is a perfect heart, the lung God made is a perfect lung. It may help to realize this better when one knows that the physical vibration of heart or lung is the same wherever the manifestation of heart or lung takes place, whether it is in an animal, a bird, or a man. It shows the universality of the idea of heart or lung and helps him to realize that when he declares for the oneness of any Divine Idea, he is declaring the Truth about that Idea.

The practitioner, then, treats of the oneness of manifestation, and it is about this oneness that he makes his declaration, always declaring that this oneness is true about his patient. It would not be enough to say the Heart of God is perfect and there is only One Heart, but he must complete this statement by saying, "This Heart of God is the heart of this patient. Nothing ever happened to it, it didn't enlarge; there was never any tension around it, there was never any pain in it; it never caused pain and there never was any emotional state that caused it to pain. It was never repressed, depressed, or suppressed. It was never tired or worn out, it never broke down, and the whole circulatory system, being a part of the Divine Life Impulse, never was impaired."

Heart is a Divine Idea and the Heart of Reality is the heart of this particular person whom you are treating. The Divine Reality must be considered as perfect, complete, ever-present, always active, ever-available, and the negation of this must be reversed in the mind of the practitioner; that is, the denial of it must be understood to have no power.

Thus the spiritual practitioner converts things into thoughts. He can think not only of *our Father which art in heaven,* but also of our perfect body and perfect organism which are in the Kingdom of Reality now, and to the practitioner this must be an intense reality. He must believe what he says. He must understand that the Kingdom of Heaven is at hand. He cannot do this unless he contradicts much that is experienced. Mentally he never deals with a material condition or a diseased condition, but he knows that since Spirit is the only Power there is, there is no mind which has been hypnotized into believing that there is or can be any opposite to Spirit.

The practitioner must know that Creative Mind hears and answers his thought because Creative Mind is ever-present. He knows that right idea is the operation of true Principle, whether it be in the science of mathematics or the Science of Mind. The Principle cannot help hearing. The mind which makes the request is the Mind which fulfills the desire, since there is but One Mind. If the practitioner can bear in mind that what he is destroying is belief, he will do well.

Now right here the uninstructed will say, "Do you mean to tell me that I do not experience discord or disease?" We do not deny that man experiences discord or disease. What we affirm is that the experience is the belief in form and that the disintegration of the belief will produce a corresponding disintegration of the form. That is why we so continuously say: *Turn things into thoughts and heal the thought.* In mental practice the practitioner must deal with belief or with thought, and he must deal with form as though it were belief and thought, else, as we have already stated, how can he conceive that thought can reach that which is not of the nature of mind, thought, or thinking?

For instance, if someone should draw a picture of a horse on a blackboard, and others seeing it should believe it to be a horse, it still would be nothing other than a picture. Now you come along and take an eraser and rub out the picture. Where is the horse? It was never a thing in itself, it only appeared to be an entity. Your knowledge that it could be rubbed out and your act of rubbing it out were but two ends of the same thing. So the mental practitioner must realize that his argument or his realization rubs out the argument of negation which projects discord. He cannot do this unless he understands that the projection of the discord is just as much a thing of thought as what he calls the thought behind such projection.

It is perhaps a little difficult to make this clear, but it means that the practitioner works in a field of mind and thought alone, and all he has to neutralize is thought, never things. It is one of the most subtle parts of this entire system of practice, one to which we should pay the most careful attention. For the root of all evil is in mental conviction, not in evil itself. The axe of Truth has to be laid at the root of evil and the false condition chopped away, so to speak. Therefore spiritual enlightenment in the mind heals the body because the body is mind in form and because spiritual enlightenment changes the form of thought in mind.

If this is true there is no adversary, no opponent, no opposition. When in the mental argument a practitioner reaches the place where he perceives or understands the Truth of his argument, his argument ceases as argument and begins as realization. It has passed from analysis into conclusion. It is this realization which is the creative power in treatment. And what is it that is to be realized? The perfection of the patient, the perfection of all people, the harmony of the condition. Furthermore, whether one is treating to heal physical disorders or treating to heal financial disorders, or any other disorders, the operation of the Principle is identical.

Substance is supply. There is but one Substance, this Substance is Omnipresent, It is right where the need appears to be, and It meets the need according to the acceptance of the one who experiences the need. It could do neither more nor less than this. One must accept supply if Substance is to interpret Itself as supply in one's experience. The practitioner realizes the Omnipresence of Substance, hence the ever-availability of supply.

This in no way turns Spirit into matter, nor does it materialize Spirit. It merely gives form to Substance. As the physical universe has been likened to the Meditation of God, so our individual experiences may be likened to our meditations of life. And our meditations of life are our awareness, our realization — an inner feeling and conviction which transcends the experience taking place in an objective world. From the standpoint of practice, there is but one Substance, but this Substance is forever active as supply. Just as there is but one Heart, which is forever active as perfect circulation and perfect impulsion, so there is one Substance forever operating as supply.

The practitioner does not necessarily need to treat his patient for specific things. He realizes the activity of Substance in the experience of his patient, and that whatever mental equivalent his patient has will automatically be filled. It is well that we understand this, because it is self-evident that the patient brings his bowl of acceptance with him. In other words, he has thoughts and desires which he wishes to have fulfilled, which are personal to him and individual with him. The practitioner pours his realization of abundance over the entire situation, and wherever there is a mold it is automatically filled, for since Substance is Omnipresent It can fill all molds without depleting Itself.

So the practitioner declares that there is but one Substance and his patient's need is supplied out of this Substance today — whatever his patient needs, everything he needs, and all that he needs is amply supplied. The limitless activity of the Infinite now manifests in form in this man's experience. His activity always produces good results; it always produces abundance because Infinite Substance is limitless supply.

Now this Substance cannot be depleted. It remains exactly what It is and Its nature is to flow forever. Therefore, wherever there is an acceptance there is a manifestation. Wherever there is a belief which inhibits manifestation, the manifestation is limited to the acceptance. That is, through unbelief we still believe in a limited form of that which we deny. The practitioner treats the form of lack as a belief in lack. He heals the belief. He works to know that Substance is Omnipresent, is forever flowing into the experience of his patient as supply, as right action.

The patient himself brings the mold of money or house, of automobile or a suit of clothes, of position or environment. The practitioner does not have to supply the mold for his patient. To assume that he has to do so would be to assume that he must take control of his patient's thought, which would be an attempt to hypnotize his patient. Naturally, he would be unsuccessful.

The practitioner does not supply the mold of thought for his patient in any instance. He merely realizes that the mold which his patient supplies is filled by the Substance which forever flows into form. Therefore the practitioner has no personal responsibility. It is his business to realize the flow of Substance; it is the privilege of the patient to receive that Substance in the form of his own desire.

BIBLES OF THE WORLD

*Fragments from the spiritual history of the race revealing
the fundamental Unity of religious thought and experience.*

JUDAISM and CHRISTIANITY

Canst thou by searching find out God? Canst thou find out the Almighty unto perfection? It is as high as heaven . . . The measure thereof is larger than the earth, and broader than the sea.

As for God, his way is perfect; the word of the Lord is tried; he is a buckler to all those that trust in him.

One God and Father of all, who is above all, and through all, and in you all.

TAOISM

There is no end or beginning to the Tao.

As soon as it proceeds to action, it has a name. When it once has a name, (men) can know to rest in it. When they know to rest in it, they can be free from all risk of failure and error.

ZOROASTRIANISM

Demand of me, thou upright one! Of me, who am the Maker, the best of all beings, the most knowing, the most pleased in answering what is asked of me; demand of me, that thou mayst be the better, that thou mayst be the happier.

To Atar — the God who is a full source of Glory, the God who is a full source of healing.

MITHRA-RELIGION

For from the Paternal Source naught that's imperfect spins (or wheels).

For the Self-begotten One, the Father-Mind, perceiving His own works, sowed into all Love's Bond . . . so that all might continue loving on for endless time, and that these weavings of the Father's Gnostic Light might never fail. With this Love, too, it is the Elements of Cosmos keep running.

MOHAMMEDANISM

And he had no host to help him instead of God, neither was he able to help himself. Protection in such a case is of God — the Truth: He is the best rewarder, and He bringeth to the best issue.

But God will bring untruth to naught, and will make good the truth by His word; for He knoweth the very secrets of the breast.

LESSON 8

INDIVIDUAL AND UNIVERSAL SUBJECTIVE

Absolute First Cause and Relative Experience

A Message from Ernest Holmes

This lesson deals with unity and multiplicity. It sounds simple, but is one of the most profound thoughts the human mind ever has entertained. It is necessary for us to realize that there is unity at the center of everything, and multiplicity and variety at the circumference. There are many people but only One Person. We are people; God or Spirit is the One Person. There are many manifestations of life, but only One Cause back of all.

Because this is true, freedom and bondage are at the center of our own consciousness, since freedom and bondage are made of the same thing. We must always keep in mind that the Original Creative Cause is at the center of our own being. That is where we use It. We are mediums between Absolute First Cause and relative experience; between the Power that makes all things, and the things that It makes for us. The original meaning of the word husband-man, *so often referred to in the Bible, is* a distributor of the Divine Gifts, one who distributes them.

As you study this lesson try to realize more fully that you are not dealing with two powers but with the varied operations of One Power. You are not dealing with two minds but with different ideas in the Mind Principle. We know that this thought will interest you, as it does all who have entertained it.

And again may we ask if you are daily following our suggestions and actually working for yourself and someone else?

May all good be with you.

INDIVIDUAL AND UNIVERSAL SUBJECTIVE
Absolute First Cause and Relative Experience

(textbook reference: pages 98-102)

In the Science of Mind we learn theoretically to substitute ideas for objects. The objective body, whether we think of it as a planet or as our own physical being, is an effect. This does not mean that we deny the physical body. Rather, we affirm a Spiritual Principle which projects the physical body.

To deny the reality of the physical body would be to affirm that we live in a world of illusion. We do not believe that the illusion is in the object, as though the object were unreal; we believe that if there is any illusion it is in our interpretation of the object.

On page 599 under the heading *Illusion* you will find this thought: *Nature is the great no-thing, yet it is not exactly nothing.* This saying from the teachings of Plotinus, one of the greatest spiritual thinkers of all ages, who lived and taught about A.D. 150, does not deny the objective world; it merely affirms that the physical world is not a self-knowing entity. For instance, the tree does not know that it is a tree, the mountain does not know that it is a mountain, the lake does not know that it is a lake.

The physical world has an actual existence but it is not a thing in itself. It is a definite form within a comprehending Mind. Because you and I live in the Mind which projects the physical world we are able to perceive what this Mind, which is also within us, has projected into form. How could you and I recognize each other unless there were one common medium of Mind or Intelligence between us? It is upon this Principle of the Universality of Mind and Intelligence that our entire science rests.

As we have stated, the illusion is not in the thing but in our interpretation of it. To say that the body is unreal would be a mistake, but it would be equally as great a mistake to say that the body is a thing in itself. We must become accustomed to the thought that there is a projector as well as a form projected. The form is real, but it is real only as a form. Further interpretation of this point will be found on page 594 under *Form: First in the chain of Causation is the Word, and this Word is conscious of Itself.* Then there follows an explanation of how this Word takes form. This should be carefully thought out.

On page 594 read the definitions of *Formless* and *Formless Substance.* They explain how Creative Mind gives form to the ideas with which It is impregnated. You will readily see that form is temporary but Mind is eternal. The body or any physical form is as real as it is supposed to be, but it is never a thing in itself. The physical body exists that the soul may function on this plane, and when by reason of any experience it is no longer possible for it to function on this plane, then the Spirit severs itself from this particular form and passes to a new one.

Our definition of *Body,* page 577, says, *The entire manifestation of Spirit, both visible and invisible, is the Body of God.* The manifestation of Spirit in form is what we mean by Body, whether that form is the human body or any other physical manifestation. It seems probable that the human body is an objective counterpart of an ethereal body.

Under the heading *Immortal Clothing,* page 491, you will find a more extensive explanation of the idea that there is a body within a body, and that we are not unclothed, but *clothed upon.* We are to know no man after the flesh but only after the Spirit; which means that we are to realize that the real man is made of the essence of pure Spirit, is some part of God. The real man has consciousness. To be conscious he must be conscious of something; hence he must be clothed in form. Therefore upon whatever plane he may be functioning, he must have a body. This body is an outward manifestation of his inner realization of life. Turn to page 492 for an explanation of *The Inner Man* and his relation to the world of effect or body.

Body means more than mere physical form and more than just invisible essence. It means the invisible essence taking form. From this viewpoint consciousness is not confined to the body, while the body is confined to consciousness. Consciousness or the Indwelling Spirit is more than any particular body. It is interesting to note the theory now accepted by some, that our physical bodies change in their entirety at least once a year. From this standpoint no living person has a bodily form which is even a year old.

We must not confuse this thought with a denial of the body, for we are not living in a world of illusion but of realities. We need never deny fact in order to affirm faith. To think of the physical world as a picture is probably correct, but the picture is real as such. It is projected, however, upon the screen of experience through some interior and invisible process of thought, of consciousness, of will, of imagination, and of feeling.

We are now ready to discuss that which changes (page 100). Since Spirit cannot change, as we have already affirmed, and since we are living in an objective world which continuously changes, we are compelled to draw the conclusion that it is only the effect that changes. If you turn to the top of page 588 you will find the statement that effect is that which follows cause, and that Causation is pure Spirit and absolute Intelligence; hence both cause and effect are in reality spiritual — they are two ends of the same thing.

If we can comprehend the meaning of spiritual ideas, such as peace or joy, we shall certainly be able to demonstrate peace and joy in our experience through a conscious use of the Law of Cause and Effect. To say that the Law of Cause and Effect works in a mental medium is correct. You as an individual are the one who uses this Law of Cause and Effect, imparting to Its impersonal but creative nature the inspiration of your thought. When this inspiration is definitely directed toward specific purposes its creativeness is unlimited and can solve all human problems.

The purpose of the study of the Science of Mind is to impart a conscious knowledge of mental principles and a definite technique for practicing them. The greatest good that can come to any person is to know that he can help himself and others without attempting to go outside himself. The eternal activity of the Spirit produces an eternal creation, ever-changing forms within the Formless.

In the last two lines on page 100 you will find this statement: *Form comes and goes but it is not self-knowing.* Since all forms are as real as they are supposed to be, even the form of disease or discord need not be considered an illusion, but the result of a wrong conclusion about life. When we come to see that discord and disease are a result of wrong thinking, would it not follow that to change the thought would result in automatically projecting a new effect?

A further development of this idea is found in the second paragraph on page 416 — the chief characteristic of subjective Law. A new contemplation will produce a new form. The question is not can a new form be projected, but can a better idea be conceived — an idea of harmony, of truth, and of beauty. The problem lies in our consciousness and not in the Law Itself.

We must not think of any particular form as evil because it brings pain instead of pleasure, for the Mind within us must be expressed; this is Its nature and we can never beat Nature at her own game. The question is, what form shall we express? Upon what idea shall we meditate? How much Good can we conceive? Do we really believe that Love overcomes hate? Have we a complete acceptance that Peace heals confusion or that Faith casts out fear? If we have, then we take our place as beneficent agents in the Divine Creative Order.

It seems impossible for us to arrive at a very great use of Spiritual Power unless we first arrive at the highest concept of Good. It seems necessary that Nature be protected from any seriously wrong use of her laws. Therefore we should expect the destructive use of these laws to destroy the instrument of such use, temporarily at least, until through experience one learns the lesson of Cause and Effect, that *whatsoever a man soweth, that shall he also reap.*

Just as form is never a thing in itself, so time is never a thing of itself. Both form and time are creations of the imagination projected upon the screen of experience. In the Cosmos the entire physical manifestation, which we call the Body of God, is a projection of the dynamic thought of the Infinite Thinker.

Let us consider anew the idea of Cause and Effect as found on page 101. All effect is subjective to its cause. These simple but meaningful words explain why it is possible for us to demonstrate health, happiness, and success. All effect is subjective to its cause. In other words, nothing in our external world projects itself. Our individual world is projected by the mind that conceived it. When this mind withdraws its contemplation from any object, that object begins to disintegrate, whether it is the physical body when the soul has deserted it, or the body of our affairs when the Creative Mind no longer thinks them into existence, or holds them in the form which Its thought has already given to them.

From this viewpoint every man carries his own destiny in his own mind, so to speak, but he does not know it, and most people would not believe it if one were to tell them. We can speak only to those who are willing to believe. It is written: *But as many as received him, to them gave he power to become the sons of God, even to them that believe on his name* (John 1:12). The philosophy that Jesus taught was one which necessitates belief in an invisible Principle. Recall how he said, *Do you believe?* or *Believe and it shall be done.*

Jesus certainly implied that there is a Power which can, does, and must act, but Its action for us is limited to our belief. That is, the effect is subjective to its cause. If we have thought poverty until everywhere we look we see it, we have surrounded ourselves with an atmosphere and an environment of impoverishment. It seems as though we are caught by an inexorable foe, but we are not. It is written: *A man's foes shall be they of his own household.* You will find a more complete explanation of this subject on page 431 under the heading *The Secret of Prayer.*

Nothing can happen to us unless it happens through us. This sounds simple enough, and yet it penetrates the very depths of Creative Causation. Nothing can happen to us unless it happens through us, since every effect is subject to its cause. It may not be easy to sense a happy environment when we are in the midst of unhappiness, but this is what we shall be called upon to do. We may be certain that the Law of the Universe is for us, and that there is nothing against us but ourselves. We must reverse the order in which we have been using the Creative Principle.

Again let us realize that the Creator is greater than His creation. Always the artist is greater than his art. Always the thinker is more than his thought. If he were not, his thought would engulf him, so to speak, and there would be no thinker left. It is a wonderful relief to know that we do have the power to turn within and meet the Creative Cause, even though we do not use this Power to the fullest extent of Its ability to accomplish for us. The creator is always greater than his creation, and if thought creates, by the same process it can re-create. To know that that which molds can re-mold, that which projects can withdraw, that which integrates form can disintegrate it, is to know the way to freedom.

Now let us consider that in the idea with which we impregnate the Creative Mind there is involved everything necessary to produce the desired results. Moreover, once the process of involution is set in motion, evolution is certain. What does this mean? It means, for instance, that if an author is writing a play and he declares that he wants a certain character to form in his mind, by his declaration he actually creates the character which now must project itself on the screen of his imagination. It is a mental creation.

When an idea makes a demand upon Mind we are dealing with the principle of involution; we are invoking the Divine Creative Mind for a specific purpose. The Law being plastic, impersonal but creative, It must at once begin to create a form like the idea involved, and through a process of evolution It presents the form to us. Thus our ideas come back to us in form, for what the Spirit involves must evolve. In our system of thought we never deny the principle of evolution. We merely say that evolution is an effect of involution. We believe that evolution and involution are the two great Principles of the Universe; that one balances the other.

In practical work this means that when you give a treatment there is already contained within it a picture of the form which is to be projected, and that the projection of the form is in the nature of an effect. The effect must follow the cause, mathematically. Evolution must follow involution mechanically. Man is a Principle of involution, and we might say he is some part of all the Principle of evolution. It is impossible for him to think without creating some form, and if he wishes to consciously control his destiny he must control his thoughts, mental states, and states of consciousness, which of course are largely subjective.

Subjective thought is the only medium between the Absolute and the relative. On the subjective side of life we are always projecting forms into the invisible, and this invisible Creative Medium is always returning some condition to us. We call the condition good or bad, big or little, better or best, but it is always some form of thought.

INDIVIDUAL AND UNIVERSAL SUBJECTIVE

If thought could not be controlled, then the Universe would be caught in Its own trap. Then would the potter become subjective to his clay. Then would the Creator have been lost in His creation. Happily such is not the case. That which molds can re-mold, that which forms can re-form, that which creates can re-create. Let us learn to create after the pattern of harmony, peace, wholeness, and abundance.

SUMMARY

Everything we see objectively is an effect of a subjective and spiritual Cause. We do not deny the varied effects; we do affirm a Unitary Cause.

We are not living in a world of illusion but of evolution, and in a certain sense everything is as real as we make it. We never deny the physical body or the physical environment. We merely affirm that we have this physical body and experience this physical environment because we are one with the Mind that projects both.

All created things come and go, for this is the play of Life upon Itself, but the Mind that projects them is constant and changeless.

One of the great secrets of this science and the thing that should perhaps appeal to our imagination more than anything else is the thought that when we treat the physical body or work to change our environment we never go outside ourselves. The *Secret Place of the Most High* is within.

Within you is Something that observes the change of Life, but the Thing within you that observes the change is changeless.

Since the Law of Mind is not an entity in Itself, that is, It is a Doer and not a Knower, and since It responds to your thinking, the answer to all problems is in consciousness.

All Causation is subjective; it is within and beneath the surface in which all objective forms are rooted. It is because of this that we have the possibility of freedom. And because these things are so, and because the Law responds to us at the level of our own inward awareness and affirmation, it follows that we must believe not only in the Spirit and the Law but in our own ability to imbibe the Spirit and use the Law.

QUESTIONS

Brief answers to these questions should be written out by the student after studying this lesson, and the answers compared with those in the Appendix.

1. What do we mean when we say we substitute ideas for objects?

2. Do we deny the physical body or physical universe?

3. What do we affirm about the physical body and physical universe?

4. How can we be conscious of physical facts and their invisible cause?

5. Why do we have physical bodies?

6. Why is some type of form or creation necessary to consciousness?

7. How is our world of experience projected?

8. What do we mean when we say only effect changes?

9. (a) How shall we consciously use the great Law of Cause and Effect?
   (b) Where do we contact this Law of Cause and Effect?

10. Does disease, lack, unhappiness, limitation, or any other created form have self-consciousness or self-determination?

11. How do we change undesirable forms, such as sickness, poverty, unhappiness, etc., into desirable forms, such as health, abundance, happiness, etc.?

12. (a) What do we mean by the use of Spiritual Power?
    (b) How do we arrive at the greatest use of this Power?

QUESTIONS

13. Is it right to use Spiritual Power to satisfy personal needs and desires?

14. Why is it necessary to believe in the Invisible Principle of Mind in order to consciously prove It?

15. Why is the Creative Principle limited to our belief when It operates for us?

16. What do we mean by a subjective state of thought?

17. What do we mean by the Absolute and the relative?

18. Why is our subjective state of thought the medium between the Absolute and relative in our lives?

METAPHYSICAL INTERPRETATIONS OF THE BIBLE

based on

Thomas Troward's *Bible Mystery and Bible Meaning*

THE GREAT NEGATION

Evil is never a thing in itself, and yet we could hardly deny its existence in human experience. While we know that two and two can never make five, we are aware that many mistakes are made in dealing with the principle of mathematics.

In his chapters *The Devil* and *The Spirit of Antichrist,* Troward explains that our Divine Sonship, carrying with it as it must the prerogative of self-choice, makes possible the experience of limitation. Perhaps the most difficult thing to realize in dealing with the laws of thought is the absolute neutrality of the Principle of Mind. We recognize the characteristic of neutrality in all other laws of nature, but fail to realize that mental laws are also natural laws; that there must be a Universal Creative Medium which corresponds to our thought exactly as we think it, thus making evil appear to be a thing in itself.

Troward tells us that . . . *since God alone is, the Devil is not. Since God is Being, the Devil is Non-Being.* It is a paradox to speak of nonexistence producing anything, and yet in a certain sense this is what evil is. It arises from a misunderstanding of Reality, and thus a failure to comply with Its true nature. But because our thought is creative and, as Troward says, *owing to the impossibility of ever divesting our Thought of its Creative Power, our conception of the Negative as something having a substantive existence of its own becomes a very real power indeed. . . .*

The Bible likens the power of evil to Satan, to the Devil, and to the serpent which tempted Eve. Eve stands for the feminine or Mother Principle in nature: *And Adam called his wife's name Eve; because she was the mother of all living.* The serpent is the Life Principle, and this Life Principle presents Itself to us in the form of our own experience; otherwise we could not be individuals.

The problem of evil, then, is not a problem of something which is a reality in itself, but rather a problem of coming to understand the nature of Reality. In the

THE GREAT NEGATION

Text of Taoism we read: *But how can the Tao be so obscured that there should be "a true" and "a false" in it? . . . Tao becomes obscured through the small comprehension [of the mind].* And from the Buddhistic: *For the cause of the karma which conducts to unhappy states of existence is ignorance.* From the Talmud: *Not God but ye yourselves, are the creators and supporters of moral evils. When a field is covered by weeds, shall a farmer complain of God?*

Perhaps one of the most illuminating passages of all referring to evil comes from the Gospel of John: *Ye are of your father the devil, and the lusts of your father ye will do. He was a murderer from the beginning, and abode not in truth, because there is no truth in him. When he speaketh a lie, he speaketh of his own: for he is a liar, and the father of it.* And in II Corinthians: *. . . for what fellowship hath righteousness with unrighteousness? and what communion hath light with darkness?*

The nature of Reality is such that the Law of Mind presents us with experiences which reflect the images of our thought. The Law which executes our conscious and unconscious will is neither good nor bad. It is a neutral Law. When our will, choice, decision, and action emanate from Goodness, then there is no evil. When our thought operates from a destructive motivation we create the evil we experience. This evil or devil is the one referred to as the *Not-Self which is opposed to the True Self . . . the one bending downward to matter, the other bending upward to God.* Swedenborg tells us: *Sin and the devil are one and the same.* And Bishop Wilberforce said, *The true devil against whom we have to be sober and vigilant is within man . . . the power within ourselves that makes for unrighteousness.* Campbell said, *Evil is a negative . . . it denotes the absence rather than the presence of something . . . Evil is not a principle at war with Good. Good is Being and evil is Non-Being.*

The spiritual and intellectual minds of the ages have sensed that evil is not a thing in itself, but is a self-created experience through which the soul passes on its evolutionary journey. This journey is not so much toward perfection as it is toward the recognition and realization of perfection. For instance, in spiritual mind healing we say that sickness, pain, poverty, impoverishment, want, fear, doubt, uncertainty, or any other type of negation is not a thing in itself, but a result of false belief and action.

The successful demonstration of spiritual science is based on the supposition that evil is the great No-Thing and that the knowledge of its nothingness, together with the recognition of the Allness of God, is what really heals. In a verse of antiquity we find this:

We praise Thee, O Father;
We give Thanks to Thee, O Light;
In Whom Darkness dwells not!

And in Habakkuk 1:13: *Thou art of purer eyes than to behold evil, and canst not look on iniquity.* We also have this enlightening message from the Koran: *Whatever good betideth thee is from God, and whatever betideth thee of evil is from thyself.*

The answer to the problem of evil is individuality and freedom. We are not dealing with an entity but with an illusion; an illusion that is more than mere imagination. It has been an experience so universally suffered that it seems like a solid fact. It is self-evident, as Troward says, that the Infinite could not be evil, because if It were It would not be a creative agency. It is impossible that Life can produce death or that That Which Is can be neutralized by that which is not.

If, as Troward suggests, God stands for everything that is Good, then the devil stands for everything that is opposed to Good. But since there can be no real final opposition to Good because God is One and Perfect, the power which seems opposed to Good is suppositional only. Thus the devil is not only called "a liar" but "the father of lies in whom dwells no truth at all." Troward points out with remarkable clarity of thought that we must differentiate between God the Living Spirit, and the laws of nature which have no volition of their own. For instance, would the fact that fire can burn us prove that the nature of Reality is, or contains, evil? All laws of nature are subject to two kinds of use. The wrong use of any of these laws produces suffering, which we call evil, until through suffering we come to righteousness. Hence even though evil is not a thing in itself, the wrong use of the Law, which automatically causes us to suffer, becomes, as the Apostle suggested, *the schoolmaster to bring us unto Christ,* that is, to a true understanding of our sonship.

Troward tells us that *the Power of the Negative . . . has its root in our denial of the Affirmative.* This does not mean that illusion is created out of Reality but that the mirror of life will reflect those conditions and situations which we continuously affirm to be true. In this way evil becomes a denial of Good; the opposite of true sonship.

It does not follow that what we call the material universe is evil, for nothing is evil in itself. It is the use of things which makes them evil. We certainly will make a limited use of things until we acquire a less limited idea of Life and of our relationship to the Supreme Spirit. We are brought back to the proposition that we must recognize Life as the Supreme Good, the supreme evil, or a mixture of each. We cannot serve God and mammon. If we would come to the Spirit for healing we must turn from everything which denies the Divine Presence. *Let him eschew evil and do Good; let him seek peace and ensue it . . . He who knoweth me, unborn, beginningless, the great Lord of the world, he, among mortals without delusion, is liberated from all sin.* These passages taken from the Gita are not unlike those found in our own New Testament: *Finally, brethren, whatsoever things are true, whatsoever things are honest, whatsoever things are just, whatsoever things are pure, whatsoever things are lovely, whatsoever things are of good report; if there be any virtue, and if there be any praise, think on these things* (Philippians 4:8).

Troward tells us: . . . *the whole question of the power of evil turns on the two fundamental Laws . . . the Law of Suggestion and the Law of the Creative Power of Thought.* He means by this that evil is not a thing in itself; neither "the devil" nor "a devil" are entities. Evil or devil stands for everything which acts or poses as a suppositional opposite to Good. Consequently Troward informs us that our whole mental concept should be built upon a realization of the Wholeness of Spirit; upon a conscious perception of Its Life-Givingness. We should recognize It as Love as well as Life. In Romans 8:31 we read: *If God be for us, who can be against us?* All of which is summed up as the Spirit of Christ which the Bible sets before us as the Divine Ideal of Sonship, the Universal Norm.

If living in harmony with the Creative Law of the Universe, and consciously seeking to adjust ourselves to Its Love and Its Divine Beneficence, constitutes the Spirit of Christ, then Its suppositional opposite would constitute what has been referred to as the spirit of Antichrist, that which is in opposition to Good. Not that there is any real opposite to Good, but that the very creative power of our false belief makes it appear as though there were such an opposite.

THE GREAT NEGATION

The Bible clearly states that Christ is within everyone. Riley says that *this Christ idea, like the germ or tiny seed, lies beneath the crust of materialism . . . the Divine Germ will . . . gradually unfold.* Robert Browning refers to this Christ in his great poem *Saul* where he says, *A Hand like this hand shall throw open the gate of new life to thee! See the Christ stand!*

It is written in John 3:6-7: *That which is born of the flesh is flesh . . . Ye must be born again.* Symbolically, this new birth takes place through the crucifixion and death of the lower qualities, transforming and transmuting the lower into the Higher Self. This is putting off the old man and putting on the new man which is Christ. This is what is meant in Isaiah 9:6: *For unto us a child is born, unto us a son is given. . . .* It is what Jesus meant when he said, *I am the way, the truth, and the life.* And when he said, *I am the light of the world; he that followeth me shall not walk in darkness. . . .* Again: *For as the Father hath life in himself; so hath he given to the Son to have life in himself.* Jesus tells us that as we arrive at a correct understanding we pass from death into life. In Echoes from the Gnosis, the Hymn of Jesus, we read:

> *I am a lamp to thee who seest Me.*
> *Amen!*
> *I am a mirror to thee who understandest Me.*
> *Amen!*
> *I am a door to thee who knockest at Me.*
> *Amen!*
> *I am a way to thee a wayfarer.*
> *Amen!*

The spirit of Antichrist is a suppositional opposite to all this. It is a denial of God as Peace, Joy, Union, Love; an affirmation of power as hate, unhappiness, disunion, and any and every other name that stands for the incarnation of evil. The Bible sums up this whole category of negation under the name Antichrist, which is a symbol of the adversary of the Higher Self. The Great Negation consists in making evil equal with Good, and particularly in seeking to use spiritual power for evil purposes. One is the supreme affirmation and the other the supreme denial. One builds up while the other tears down.

Human experience teaches us that the more definite our knowledge of the laws of nature, the more destructive we may become unless Divine Wisdom attends such knowledge. There is a vast difference between knowledge and wisdom, for knowledge pertains to the nature of laws; wisdom to their proper uses. For example, if the money spent in destructive purposes in the last quarter of a century had been spent instead for constructive ends, it would have eliminated any necessity for poverty throughout the world.

Again we might ask ourselves why the Divine and Beneficent Spirit, or God, permits such destruction? And again we come back to the answer given us from the enlightened throughout the ages, and which Jesus so plainly symbolized in the story of the Prodigal Son. Man is let alone to discover his own nature and to suffer the experience of any misuse of that nature. From the Cup of Monad we gather this saying: *God's image hath been sketched for thee . . . if thou wilt attentively dwell on it . . . that image shall become thy guide.* In II Corinthians 3:18: *But we all, with open face beholding as in a glass the glory of the Lord, are changed into the same image from glory to glory. . . .* Even God cannot give us what we refuse to accept. Thus we create evil through the mistaken conception that Good is divided against Itself. This is the Great Negation.

Reference to the spirit of Antichrist does not mean that there is a real Antichrist. It refers only to the wrong use of the laws of our being and the consequent suffering which such wrong use imposes upon us. Troward tells us: *The temple which is profaned [by the wrong use of the law] is the innermost sanctuary of our own heart. And . . . it is of the utmost importance who is enthroned there.*

Are we enthroning Love, Wisdom, Truth, and Beauty? Is the altar of our faith erected before the one true and only God, and Christ, the one true and only Son, already within us? Or is it erected before that which denies this eternal Unity of Good and which affirms that each man is for himself; that power alone is worthwhile? Power uncontrolled by love is chaos. Is our altar erected to chaos in the midst of our own confusion? Or do we believe in an All Supreme Wisdom and permit It to govern us?

In no way would this belittle or render futile our individuality. We should merely be using It for righteous or right purposes. The Law would still be our servant, but our use of It would be on the side of right. Troward states: *The greater the power you put into anyone's hands, the more mischief will result if through ig-norance of its true uses he misapplies it.* Therefore the sacred scriptures of the ages warn us that the gateway to Reality is narrow and the road is straight. *On this [road] proceeds he who knows Brahma; he has been a doer of the good whose nature is like light.* This quotation taken from the Upanishads is not unlike one from Proverbs: *But the path of the just is as the shining light, that shineth more and more unto the perfect day.*

It is interesting that in warning us against the uses of evil the ancient scrip-tures have never assumed that evil is a thing in itself. It has always been called the great No-Thing. That is, the great Nothing in Itself, the illusion, because the deep thinkers of all times have perceived that Reality must be One, even though this One manifests in multiplicity.

Jesus sums up the whole spirit of worship in the simple phrase that it should be done in Spirit and in Truth. Troward tells us: *The essence and not the form is what counts, because the whole thing is a question of mental attitude.* We are to realize that there is but one Infinite Creative Agency in the Universe; it is God, the Living Spirit Almighty. There is also a Law in the Universe which obeys the will of God and of man. The Spirit is the very essence of Truth and Goodness; the Law is the actor. The Spirit is Love; the Law is Power. The Law of Mind, like the law of electricity or any other law in nature, is entirely neutral and im-personal, just as the creative soil is entirely neutral and impersonal. We personify It through the use we make of It. This use may be what we call evil, but from the standpoint of Reality Itself the only final use we could make of this Law would be the use of Goodness, since any other use of It would merely destroy its own embodiment. This is the only power evil has.

Back of the Law is the spirit of Goodness, the spirit of Inspiration, Divine Guidance, etc. Both Christ and Antichrist are ways of using the Law of Cause and Effect. The Spirit of Christ is the spirit of one who uses It in Divine Love and Wisdom. Thus Power, obeying Love and Wisdom, produces happiness, peace, and joy without harm to anyone. But the use of power uncontrolled by love and wisdom produces transitory discord. Whether or not we choose to call this an illusion makes no dif-ference; it is most certainly a human experience.

We must not hesitate to use the Law of Mind for fear of suffering a negative consequence, for always we shall be using It constructively if there is nothing in our use of It which denies Good. The most simple-minded can differentiate between the two. It is never right to use the Law of Mind to influence anyone, to control anyone, to suggest anything to anyone. It is always right to use It to help, to uplift, to heal, to make happy, to bless.

Troward tells us that the Law of Mind, which has been called Anima Mundi, is not the originating Principle, but is the avenue through which this Principle works. Medieval writers referred to It as the Universal Medium, esoterically called Water, just as they spoke of Animus Dei, signifying the Divine Spirit, and they were careful to discriminate between the two. Troward simplifies such expressions by calling the Universal Creative Medium the subconscious Mind of the Universe, which by Its nature affords a matrix for the germination of the seeds of thought that are planted in It.

MENTAL TECHNIQUE FOR SPIRITUAL TREATMENT

Unless there were a definite method of procedure in spiritual mind healing it could not be considered scientific. Unless a definite technique could be delivered there would be no intelligent approach to the subject. Unless one could learn this technique and consciously apply it, it would not be universally applicable. But the Science of Mind is just as definitely scientific and just as positively based on an actual principle as in any other science.

The fact that we are dealing with invisible forces makes them no more intangible than any other force of nature with which we deal. All life is invisible, all energy is invisible, all causation is invisible. The Principle of Mind is invisible and Its practice is invisible, but Its results are the Word made flesh.

Since the modern approach to mental science has developed simultaneously along both the psychological and metaphysical fronts it is well to analyze our position and determine where we agree with the psychological method and where we depart somewhat from it. For whether or not we are conscious of the fact, we more or less combine both methods.

Unfortunately, many people in the metaphysical field do not understand this, and in their ignorance of the subject deny psychology a place in their system, and just as unfortunately many psychologists do not understand the metaphysical viewpoint, and in their ignorance deny its place in their field. With the broader understanding of both fields there will be a more conscious cooperation, for each in its own way is seeking to help and to be helped.

The approach of psychology to mental healing has already passed through several distinct stages. Starting with mesmerism it developed into hypnotism; next into mental suggestion; and finally into mental explanation, which is the method employed by most psychologists; that is, if we reduce their methods to the simplest interpretations.

Neither psychiatry nor analytical psychology is hypnotic, nor do they practice mental suggestion. Their entire field is one of explanation. In analytical psychology the explanation is drawn from the patient's consciousness in such a way that he self-sees his trouble, and by this self-seeing the difficulty is supposed to be dissipated.

In the earliest stages of analytical psychology it was thought necessary that the analyst should draw out of the consciousness of his patient every trivial incident which might have led to his mental and physical undoing. This has made of analysis one of the most subtle of arts, as well as one of the most difficult practices. If one expects to draw out of the consciousness of one's patient the most trivial incidents of his life, the method becomes painstaking, laborious, and more or less cumbersome; generally the treatment must cover a long period of time.

There is a tendency today among many practicing analysts and psychiatrists to short-cut this method somewhat, and to drain more quickly the psychic confusion from the unconscious memory of the patient, thus producing a quicker response.

In spiritual mind healing we do not have to uncover every unconscious cause of mental confusion with its attendant physical distress. We know that broad, generalized statements often effect a healing of disease without either the practitioner or the patient having any specific knowledge of its cause. We know that the clearer one's consciousness is and the more definitely certain one is that Spirit is the Absolute Cause of all, and that Good alone governs, the more quickly will healing take place. We know that silent recognition and realization elevate the consciousness to a place of greater power and make possible a more immediate manifestation. Jesus did not analyze; he announced.

In actual practice we combine analysis with realization. Sometimes we use one and sometimes the other, but more often we combine the two. It is probably safe to say that, in most practice, the combination of these two methods has been more effective than the use of one to the exclusion of the other. No one appears to be in a continual state of conscious Spiritual Power, but we all have the capacity to give scientific mental treatments. We must resort to our definite technique for practice, and through mental statements arrive at a spiritual conclusion, a consciousness of the Allness of God and the ever-present availability of Good.

We claim to have a science which can be delivered to all intelligent persons, and we claim that the average person can effectively use this science provided he complies with its Principle and Law.

It is therefore necessary to deliver a definite technique and a conscious method for procedure. That is why we start with the proposition of Perfect God, Perfect Man, and Perfect Being. This is the spiritual Principle which the mind, through right ideas, seeks to demonstrate, and in so doing it will probably combine argument with realization. Just what do we mean by argument in mental treatment? We mean the phases of thought through which the mind goes to arrive at a conclusion. The following example may help to clarify this point:

A person suddenly finds himself feeling greatly discouraged and mentally depressed. He knows that God is neither discouraged nor depressed. He knows that nothing has happened to the Divine Reality. He might, by sitting in quiet contemplation for a few moments, so fill himself with this Spirit of Reality that his negation would disappear as mist before the sun. This of course would be the ideal way. But suppose in contemplating this he fails. His next step is to resort to his mental technique. He begins to make definite statements, similar to the following:

God is neither sad nor depressed. There is not life apart from God; therefore my life is God. Consequently I am neither sad nor depressed. God is not afraid of anything. My mind and the Mind of God are One Mind; therefore my mind cannot entertain fear.

At this place in his treatment, the image of fear or some memory of fear may arise. Immediately he would say:

This fear is not person, place, or thing. It has no law to support it, no power to uphold it, no consciousness to conceive it, no law to enforce it, no person to express it.

He would be repudiating the negation, and would follow such repudiation by the affirmation:

My mind is the Mind of God — calm and peaceful, unafraid and certain. All Presence, all Power, all Peace, and Joy are mine today. I am not afraid of anything because I now see that there is nothing to be afraid of. The images of fear cannot operate through me. I am completely separated from any belief in fear. I do not remember anything in the past of which I was afraid. I do not anticipate anything in the future of which I shall be afraid, and I am not conscious of anything going on today of which

MENTAL TECHNIQUE FOR SPIRITUAL TREATMENT

I am afraid.

There is no discouragement. I am protected by the only Power there is. I live in the only Presence there is. This word completely neutralizes, obliterates, casts out, expels every thought of fear and every belief that there is anything to be afraid of.

A person making statements similar to these would probably find himself gradually lifted up mentally to the place in thought where he would begin to feel at ease. The images of doubt would no longer assail him. Calm and peace would accumulate in his thought. In such degree as he embodied the meaning of the words which he had just spoken, a sense of realization would fill his consciousness with peace. This sense of realization he should mentally hold in his consciousness for a period of time, and finally it would become permanent.

One thing, however, we must be careful to avoid, and that is fooling ourselves. Our work rests upon demonstration, and whatever method we use, how much argument we employ, or whatever state of realization we may reach, we must prove our position. We must actually demonstrate that thought manifests in form, in actual conditions, in objective life. If thought is not manifesting in this way in our experience we must work with ourselves until it does. We must never take *No* for an answer. To do so would be to repudiate the Principle in which we believe, and wreck our faith in It.

Therefore we must persist in our effort until the purpose we have in mind is accomplished in actual fact and not merely in fancy. We must always remember that proper use of the Science of Mind is not a practice through which we fall into a mental reverie as an escape from objective life. Our work is not done properly unless something happens as a result of it.

This something that happens we can always weigh and measure objectively. For instance, if we are treating someone who has high blood pressure our work is not accomplished until the patient can go to a physician for proper and thorough physical examination and receive the verdict that the blood pressure is normal.

Treatment is not for the purpose of helping us either to avoid reality or to endure unhappy situations. It is for the express purpose of changing situations, and unless situations or conditions are changed as a result of the treatment, we have missed the mark. Always we must insist that we demonstrate our proposition, for our motto is: *To do is to know, and to know is to do.*

BIBLES OF THE WORLD

Fragments from the spiritual history of the race revealing
the fundamental Unity of religious thought and experience.

BUDDHISM

If you see a wise man, like a guide to treasure-trove, pointing out your faults and failings, follow him. Such company brings prosperity.

CONFUCIANISM

Heaven protects and establishes us, so that in everything we may prosper.

When you find wealth within your reach, do not try to get it by improper means; do not seek for more than your proper share.

HINDUISM

Thou, Lord of wealth, art Master of all treasures.

JUDAISM and CHRISTIANITY

But the fruit of the Spirit is love, joy, peace, longsuffering, gentleness, goodness, faith, meekness, temperance; against such there is no law.

Wherefore, if God so clothe the grass of the field, which today is, and tomorrow is cast into the oven, shall he not much more clothe you, O ye of little faith?

But let him ask in faith, nothing wavering. For he that wavereth is like a wave of the sea, driven with the wind and tossed.

ISLAM

It is God Who hath created the heavens and the earth, and Who hath sent down the waters from the heaven, and so bringeth forth the fruits for your food.

SIKHISM

At the beginning and the end God is ever our Helper.

God is immortal, undecaying, imperishable, and of changeless purpose, Creator of all, the Remover of sickness, sorrow, and sin.

MEDITATION

I know that the Power of Good is an underlying Principle of the Universe. It is a manifestation of God. I know that God is All-Good. I know that Good underlies all manifestations of thought and form, because Good is all there is. Good is at the root of all manifestation, regardless of Its seeming absence.

I know that this Good is the basic Principle of my existence. That which I Am is Good. I know that Good is the Law of my being. It is the vital, living Force that supports my every harmonious thought and deed. There is no other power, for God is Good and there cannot be God and something else. God is in all; and God is Good.

I know there is nothing in me that could possibly obstruct or withhold the Divine Circuit of Life and Love, which Good is. My word dissolves every negative thought or impulse that could throw a shadow over my perfection.

Good flows through me to all. Good shines through my thoughts and actions. Good harmonizes my body so that it is revitalized and manifests perfection in every cell, in every organ, in every function. Good harmonizes my mind so that Love sings joyously in my heart, and I am completely conscious of All-Good in me, around me, and in all that is.

I am in complete Unity with my Good.

APPENDIX

These questions and answers were compiled by Dr. Reginald Armor. Dr. Armor was a charter member of the Board of Trustees of the Institute of Religious Science and Philosophy (now known as Ernest Holmes College), as well as Associate Minister with Dr. Holmes.

His love for and dedication to the Principles of this course established him as a highly respected and successful Practitioner. As Director of the Institute he guided the Home Study Course to international recognition. In addition he served, until his transition, as Associate Minister and Practitioner with Dr. William Hornaday, Minister of Founder's Church.

ANSWERS
Lesson 1

1. God never had a beginning. God has always existed and always will. *In the beginning God* means the beginning of any creative series. Any creative series begins in and emerges from God.

2. We think of God as Infinite Mind or Intelligence in and through all creation. We may think of God as Nature, and embodying all the laws of Nature. In our system of thought God is All in All. He is immanent in All and is everywhere present. Our conclusion is that we are unified with and at one with God, for if God is the All in All, then He must be in us.

3. A creative series means from cause to effect. All things which we see, touch, taste, and handle are effects; that is, they have a preceding cause. For every visible effect there must be an invisible cause. A creative series, then, means cause, medium, and effect. For instance, in an invention the series would be: the cause (the idea in the inventor's mind); the medium (the intelligent activity on the part of the inventor); and the effect (the result or the completed invention).

4. Yes. Any effect may be the beginning of a new creative series. For instance, the invention, or effect of the inventor, may be an electric light globe, which in turn becomes the cause of a brilliantly lighted room. Such relative causes are termed *secondary causes*.

5. We mean the First Cause which is back of everything. It is first because nothing precedes It and It is therefore Its own reason for being. Hence when we say, "In the beginning God," we mean God as First Cause. If we reason from effect back to cause we shall arrive at the necessary conclusion that pure Intelligence is the First Cause. For example, back of all figures as we use them there is a principle or law of mathematics, which is its own reason for being. All we can say about it is that it is because it is.

6. Being unified with God we are at one with First Cause; hence, First Cause is always ready to respond to us by bringing new experiences into our lives.

7. Spirit is that which knows. Therefore It is Consciousness. Spirit is the originator of all ideas. The Spirit of God creates ideas, and these ideas become things. Spirit, then, as Conscious Intelligence is the first step in any creative series. It is that Mind which knows Itself to be. The Spirit of God in operation is the movement of Intelligence (Mind) upon Itself, producing creation.

8. Since Spirit is the original Intelligence or the Mind in everything, Spirit must be present in man. The conscious knowingness of man is the Spirit of God in him. This Spirit in man is the thinker. Hence man is a creative agent. Man is a center of God's thought. There is nothing else he could be. His thought is creative because God in him is the Creator.

9. Strictly speaking, the Spirit within man is God, the Infinite Potential of all wisdom, the Source of all intelligence and ideas, and we cannot say It grows or develops. That which develops in man is a growing capacity to comprehend more life, power, and action. In this sense man's use of Spirit does develop, his power increases, and his mind expands through meditation, which is mental attention, through prayer, which is communion, and through intuition, which is God talking to him. As these mind faculties develop man evolves, or the God-idea in him expands. And right action follows right knowing.

10. If Spirit is Consciousness, and if the movement of Spirit is thought or idea, then it follows that thought is creative. We are constantly thinking, and thought is creative power, and it does create the conditions in our lives and affairs. All thought is creative, and when we realize that by our thinking we are shaping

the course of our lives, then we shall consciously direct this thought power in such a way that it will result in an orderly and happy manifestation. *As a man thinketh in his heart, so is he.*

ANSWERS
Lesson 2

1. (a) If there were two ultimate powers neither would be infinite, for if each were infinite they would neutralize each other and the result would be zero.

   (b) Scientific findings now indicate that all form comes from a common source, Universal Energy, which is undivided, has always existed, and always will exist. So we say all that is or ever shall be has as its Source one Ultimate Reality, which is Unity.

2. The created forms may be many and varied, but coming from the One Source they cannot be different in essence; hence there cannot be duality. To use an example, let us take water, which is one form of substance, and subject it to heat. The form changes as the water becomes steam. If we lower the temperature of the water it becomes solid ice, which is another form. Here we have three different forms of the one substance. The form of each is different but the essence remains the same.

3. We cannot see Ultimate Reality. We can only sense It through inner feeling. We constantly see and experience the forms of Reality. For instance, we cannot see love, beauty, harmony, etc., but we are constantly experiencing what these qualities do. The resulting forms are the outer symbols of the inner Reality. The realm of Reality is the unseen world of thought and idea that is behind the world of form which we experience.

4. The Law is a Law of Cause and Effect. Thought or idea is the invisible cause. Manifestation or the created form is the effect. The form is an outer symbol expressing the idea. Thoughts are acted upon by a Subjective Law which responds with mathematical exactness to the ideas of Spirit.

   Man may use this Law because It is an aspect of Infinite Mind and everywhere present. Hence It is present within man. Man's thought or Spirit in operation is acted upon by this Law of Cause and Effect to manifest definite conditions in his body and his affairs.

5. The Infinite, being All, cannot be depleted in any way. There is always more and still more substance, wisdom, and creative ability. The possibility of creation is limitless.

6. If any thought is creative it must follow that all thought is creative. The Law is exact, not capricious. However, since man's belief is his use of the Law, it must follow that the greater the conviction the more power his word will have. Therefore conscious prayer, treatment, or meditation is more powerful than mere idle words.

7. The answer is that our conviction is not always completely sustained. We may reach a point of acceptance during a treatment, and immediately neutralize it. In this case we have not arrived at complete conviction. We must always remember the Law is exact and cannot show favoritism.

8. In observing the Universal nature of God we view both volitional and mechanical activity. The Word of God is the engineer directing the Law of God, which in Its turn is the mechanical activity or the engine. The Word and the Law are coexistent. Before an engine can be effective there must be an engineer. Both are necessary.

9. (a) The conscious mind of man is the volitional, self-conscious faculty. It is self-conscious mind. Man thinks, forms ideas, and consciously directs the law of his life with his conscious mind. It is the engineer.

   (b) The subjective mind of man is not volitional, but mechanical. It is the law of his being. It accepts ideas and thought, and is subject to the conscious mind. It knows only to do. It is the engine which responds to the engineer.

10. No. There is only One Universal Mind with two aspects — Spirit and Law. In man's mind, we call Spirit the conscious mind and Law the subjective mind.

APPENDIX
ANSWERS
Lesson 3

1. The basic truth about any law of nature is that all natural laws have always existed.

2. We can use the laws of nature when we recognize them and understand how they work.

3. No, the Principle of Life or God does not evolve. It continuously unfolds.

4. No. The Creative Spirit does not make something out of nothing. Creation means the passing of Spirit into form. It is the play of Life upon Itself.

5. No. Man will eternally unfold. There is no limit to his possible expansion.

6. Man progresses through his discovery of natural laws and his relationship with them.

7. We do not see the spiritual realities or the principles of nature. What we see and experience are their effects.

8. (a) No. We cannot explain life.

   (b) God is revealed to us through His creation and through our own minds. We see the form but not the Spirit.

9. The main idea to keep in mind in studying this science is that God as Spirit is a Divine Presence, while the Principle of this science is a Law of Cause and Effect.

10. We use the laws of nature, first by finding out what a law is; next by cooperating with it, by complying with its mode of operation. In this way we cause it to serve us.

11. Since the laws of nature are universal and impersonal, they belong to whoever uses them.

12. The purpose of life is self-expression.

13. We glorify God by becoming emancipated from bondage.

14. Final emancipation from bondage is accomplished by unifying with the Divine Presence, by understanding Its will and cooperating with Its nature.

15. The Science of Mind is a study of life and the nature of the laws of thought.

16. By the Law and the Word we mean that Spirit, the Divine Knower, operates through a mechanical Law. This Law is Mind in Action; It is the Principle of mental science.

17. Mental healing is accomplished through a correct mental attitude toward the Truth about God and the Truth about man's real being.

18. No. Spirit as Knower is Causation. Law as Doer obeys Spirit as Knower. Hence Law as Doer is subject to Spirit as Knower. They are two attributes of the One Mind.

19. The result of conscious thought is that the mental Law responds and produces a form as the mirror reflects the image held before it.

20. No. No one ever has seen the Universal Mind. We see only what Mind does. Because we can think we know that Mind is.

21. No. It is some part of It. Man personifies the Universal Mind.

22. We increase our use of Creative Mind through a deeper realization of our Unity with the Divine Spirit.

ANSWERS
Lesson 4

1. Our ability to demonstrate Spiritual Law depends upon our belief in the use of, compliance with, and dependence on the Mental Law of Cause and Effect.

APPENDIX

2. We should think of the Principle of Spiritual Mind Healing in terms of exact Law automatically responding to Spirit.

3. We should think of the Spirit of God as a Divine Presence within and around us, personal to us and personified through us.

4. We commune with Spirit through prayer and meditation; through opening our consciousness to Its influx.

5. The burning bush symbolizes the Divine Presence in all nature.

6. Jacob's experience symbolizes that God is personal to all people, and that each comes to Him individually without the aid of mediators.

7. The angels represent the ladder of intuition or the influx of Divine Ideas into the mind of man.

8. The Subjective Law responds to us by intelligently acting upon our thought.

9. No. This Law must respond to our word and execute directions given It. The Law of Itself has no volition.

10. The power of Jesus was the result of his faith in God, and his understanding of Spiritual and Mental Law.

11. (a) We derive authority over any law through the knowledge that all laws of nature are exact. They never are things of caprice, and may be depended upon with mathematical certainty.

    (b) Yes, Mental Law, being a natural law, is like any other law of nature.

12. Mental treatment is using the Law of Mind for definite purposes.

13. Mental treatment takes place in the mind of the one treating.

14. No. *Unconscious* means without consciousness, or nonexistent. *Subconscious*

means below the threshold of, and the servant of, conscious mind.

15. Scientific mental practice is a conscious and definite use of Mental Law.

16. By the Trinity we mean cause, medium, and effect — Spirit, Law, and Form.

17. (a) No. God cannot will evil or limitation because His nature is Wholeness, and because the Will of God cannot contradict the Nature of God.

    (b) Evil is a misinterpretation of God. Limitation is a restricted concept of God.

18. In giving a mental treatment one should use the words and thoughts which convey the desired meaning to one's own mind.

ANSWERS
Lesson 5

1. By *creation* we mean the invisible world becoming visible. In the mental world, mind formulating ideas.

2. Endless creation means the Spirit eternally creating and taking form.

3. By resolving things into thoughts we mean uncovering the mental cause.

4. In mental science, resolving things into thoughts means making a mental diagnosis.

5. By mental diagnosis we mean uncovering discordant thought that it may be replaced by harmonious thought.

6. By mental correspondents we mean the images of thought behind objective experiences.

7. We use the Divine Creative Power every time we think.

8. By involution we mean placing an idea in mind as we would plant a seed in the ground.

9. By evolution we mean the act of thought taking form as the seed becomes the plant.

10. By reducing faith to science we mean understanding Spiritual Law and making conscious use of It.

11. By *entering the closet and closing the door* when we pray, we mean mentally turning from appearance and accepting the desired answer, without the necessity of knowing how it is to be brought about.

12. *Intelligence decrees and Law executes* means that the Word of Spirit (and man is Spirit) decrees and the Mental Law of Cause and Effect executes.

13. The unity of thought and imagination in treatment means that both the intellect and the feeling accept the treatment.

14. *Man as a creative center of God Consciousness* means man is individualized Spirit, and because God's thought is creative, man's thought is creative.

15. Abstract statements without specific realization and direction will not demonstrate because abstract statements are only a recognition of Law, while specific realization and direction give instruction to the Law.

16. We must make conscious use of the Creative Power of Mind; otherwise we cannot direct It for definite purposes.

17. Both cause and effect are Spiritual because they are two ends of the same thing, and because Spirit takes form, which is effect.

18. The secret of the power of Jesus was his realization of his Unity with God.

19. *Energy and intelligence moving as mathematical law* means that laws of thought, like laws of physics, are exact.

20. We get better results from mental treatment on some days than on others because sometimes our thought is clearer and our realization of its power is greater.

APPENDIX

ANSWERS
Lesson 6

1. It is the Mind of God within us that knows.

2. We use as much of the Mind of God as we are conscious of and accept.

3. By being conscious of and embodying the Mind of God, we mean an inner faith, a spiritual awareness, and a mental conviction in our thought.

4. We have all the Power and all the Good that there is to use.

5. We make prayer effective by believing that it is effective.

6. The Will of God for us is harmony, good, peace, joy, and life.

7. We should think of the Spirit as our friend and the Law as our servant.

8. The Spirit is infinite and personal to everyone because It is in everyone.

9. The Law is not personal to us. It is merely a mechanical force of nature.

10. The Spirit as Person has warmth, color, and responsiveness. The Law as Principle also responds to us, but merely as a mechanical force.

11. In dealing with God as Infinite Mind we gain, since God, being Omnipresent, is in us and personal to us.

12. Scientific mental treatment, in order to be effective and produce desired results, must be conscious, definite, and active.

13. Man's place in the creative order is to make use of and distribute the life, love, and substance of God.

14. A feeling of Divine Presence, coupled with the knowledge that the Law must respond, gives power to our word.

15. If we wish to use the Law of Cause and Effect for freedom rather than bondage we must change the image of our thought from bondage to freedom.

ANSWERS
Lesson 7

1. By the creative medium of Spirit we mean the intelligent but subjective creative Law of Mind.

2. When we use the words *intelligent but subjective* we mean that the Law of Mind which acts upon our word is creative but not selective.

3. You can direct the Mental Law for others because It is everywhere present. It is a Doer and not a knower; hence It must follow your direction.

4. Our subjective mind is the place where we use the Universal Law of Mind, which is subjective.

5. A practitioner should have confidence that his word acting through Law will do what it is supposed to do.

6. The Self-contemplation of Spirit means the Self-knowingness of God.

7. The Self-contemplation or the Self-knowingness of Spirit has a meaning identical with the Word of God.

8. The next great step which psychology must take will be the recognition that Mind is an Eternal Principle which man individualizes.

9. We use the Creative Principle every time we think.

10. New thoughts create new conditions because thought is creative, while conditions are in the realm of effect.

11. We change conditions by reversing our thought patterns, i.e., turning in thought from the undesirable, and steadfastly contemplating that which we desire.

12. Since the Universe is a Unity and not a duality, positive thoughts of Good always overcome negative beliefs in evil, such as lack, limitation, etc.

13. When we declare the Truth about someone we affirm his Spiritual nature, his Unity with Good, his Wholeness in Spirit, mind, body, and affairs.

14. A spiritual or mental treatment takes place in the thought of the one giving it.

15. The treatment given in the thought of the practitioner affects his patient because each lives in the One Mind.

16. The power of a treatment is in the conviction that the Power is already there and does not have to be concentrated but merely recognized and used.

17. In the Science of Mind we seek to demonstrate that the Spiritual Thought Force in us can overcome all forms of limitation.

18. We cannot explain the Creative Power within us, but we can recognize, accept, and make use of It.

19. Our inability to explain the Creative Power within us in no way weakens our position. No scientist will ever attempt to explain first principles; he merely accepts them.

20. The conscious, subconscious, subjective, etc., are all phases of the One Mind; hence we do not divide Mind against Itself when we use these expressions.

ANSWERS
Lesson 8

1. In mental treatment, when we substitute ideas for objects we are recognizing that all facts have a mental origin.

2. In the Science of Mind we deny neither the physical body nor the physical universe.

3. We affirm that the physical body and the physical universe are manifestations of the Mind of God. Hence the real Truth about them is Wholeness, Harmony, and Perfection.

4. We perceive physical facts and their invisible causes because we live in and are one with the Mind which conceives all ideas and projects all facts. This Mind is the Mind of God and man.

5. We have physical bodies because they are necessary for self-expression on the physical plane.

6. Form or creation is necessary to consciousness; otherwise Mind would remain unexpressed.

7. We project our world of experience through the invisible process of thought, will, imagination, and feeling.

8. When we say that effects alone change, we mean that while the world of facts, experiences, created forms, etc., changes, the Cause back of it, which is God, Mind, Spirit, or the Creative Principle, remains permanent.

9. (a) We consciously use the Law of Cause and Effect by definitely impressing our desires upon It.

   (b) We contact the Law of Cause and Effect at the center of our own being.

10. Since all created forms are but effects of the Mind Principle, they of themselves can have no self-determination.

11. We change the undesirable form into a more desirable one by consciously and definitely letting go of the idea behind the one, and mentally contemplating and accepting the idea back of the other.

12. (a) By the use of Spiritual Power we mean the most effective use of Creative Mind.

(b) We arrive at the greatest use of this Power when our thought is most completely unified with Its nature, i.e., when our thought is constructive, harmonious, and life-giving.

13. It is right to use Spiritual Power for any purpose, provided such purpose is life-giving and harms no one.

14. It is necessary to believe in the Invisible Principle of Mind in order to demonstrate, because we are living in a Mental and Spiritual Universe and because that which the mind believes in and accepts, it experiences.

15. The Creative Principle can operate for us only by operating through our belief. Hence we limit Its operation to such belief.

16. A subjective state of thought means any habitual thought pattern in a person's mind.

17. By the Absolute we mean the invisible Cause; and by the relative we mean the visible effect which depends upon this invisible Cause.

18. Our subjective state of thought is the medium between the Absolute and relative, because it contains our habitual thought patterns which are continually projecting themselves into mind.